Praise for *So Long as It's Wild*

"A grand adventure. She makes you want to ensure that you're telling a good story with your life. It's a profound thing to learn so much about your mother, who she was when she was in love and what it was like to watch her dreams crumble and new dreams emerge. And she came out on the other side even stronger. I am in awe of her and her story."

—JEDIDIAH JENKINS, *New York Times* bestselling author of *To Shake the Sleeping Self* and *Like Streams to the Ocean*

"Barbara Jenkins's unique and honest perspective of her walk across America will inspire women and girls everywhere to know that their story is worth telling."

—CONNIE BRITTON, Award-winning American actress, and star of *Dirty John*, *Friday Night Lights*, and *Nashville*

"From the swamplands of the south and across America— step by step you will be on the journey with Barbara Jenkins. Her grit and outlook on life are inspiring and bring healing and perspective to any generation. She was born a gifted soul turned writer, and her story was meant to be shared."

—BRIDGET CONNELLY, Founder/CEO Luna Bay Company

SO LONG AS IT'S WILD

SO LONG AS IT'S WILD

Standing Strong After My
Famous Walk Across America

BARBARA JENKINS

New York Times bestselling coauthor of
The Walk West and *The Road Unseen*

DEXTERITY
NASHVILLE

DEXTERITY

Dexterity, LLC
604 Magnolia Lane
Nashville, TN 37211

Printed in the United States of America.

First edition: 2023
10 9 8 7 6 5 4 3 2 1

ISBN: 978-1-947297-71-5
ISBN: 978-1-947297-72-2 (E-book)
ISBN: 978-1-947297-73-9 (Audiobook)

Publisher's Cataloging-in-Publication data
Names: Jenkins, Barbara, author.
Title: So long as it's wild : standing strong after my famous walk across America / Barbara Jenkins.
Description: Nashville, TN: Dexterity, 2023.
Identifiers: ISBN: 978-1-947297-71-5 (hardcover) | 978-1-947297-71-5 (ebook) | 978-1-947297-73-9 (audio)
Subjects: LCSH Jenkins, Barbara. | Christian biography--United States. | Walking--United States. | United States--Description and travel. | BISAC BIOGRAPHY &; AUTOBIOGRAPHY / Personal Memoirs
Classification: LCC BR1725.J389 2023 | DDC 280/.4/0922--dc23

Cover design by Notch Design
Interior design by PerfecType, Nashville TN

Dedicated to
Josephine and Lyla

God never made an ugly landscape.
All that the sun shines on is beautiful, so long as it is wild.
—John Muir

CONTENTS

CONTENTS

CONTENTS

INTRODUCTION

A group of us were enjoying a picnic lunch on a perfect fall day in Telluride, Colorado, in 2016 when my son Jed's friends, television actors Aaron and Sophia, suggested I write my story. They said it would make a great movie.

"Maybe so." I smiled.

I was sure actors said things like that to people all the time, but because of them, a seed was planted. Five years later, when my granddaughter Josephine asked if I *really* walked across America, that seed began to grow some roots.

For twenty-five years, people had asked me to write my memoir, but I didn't want to, wasn't ready, or didn't believe anyone would be interested. The story you are about to read is my version of a walk across America and my journey before and after. It is how *I* experienced people, places, and circumstances. Boxes of my handwritten journals, original notes, and thousands of slides helped me recall my adventures and untold stories, because memories can grow hazy over time. I have been silent for almost forty years, until now.

Why would a woman working on her master's degree drop everything to walk across America? The thought was outrageous. It had to be true love, pure insanity, or a higher calling, people said. They weren't entirely wrong, but they were missing something. This is a winding tale of adventure, self-discovery, and personal and spiritual growth. It is a deeply personal journey over America's prairies, under purple mountain majesties, through ecstasies and agonies to find my way. Mine are hard-earned lessons. I faced devils on the road and devils after the walk ended—not to mention devils before any of it began.

During the 1980s, I was half of America's sweetheart couple. Before the Internet, Peter Jenkins and I appeared in newspapers and magazines; we were interviewed on national radio and television stations. We were on the cover of *National Geographic*, and our story became one of the most popular in the publication's history. Money and opportunity fell out of the sky. I had never been so rich in my hillbilly life, and life with Peter was a bowl of ripe, delicious cherries. Until it wasn't and I vanished. Millions of readers captivated by our adventures in *A Walk Across America*, *The Walk West*, and *The Road Unseen* were asking, "What happened to Barbara? She walked across America too." I hope this book answers that question and more.

ONE

SO LONG AS IT'S WILD

Cajun Country, July 1976

The sun burned hot on my lily-white skin as I walked on the shoulder of the road, swatting at swamp mosquitoes and black flies. It was hard to breathe. Humidity hung in the air like cloudy white steam. Spanish moss dangled from gnarled and ancient live oak trees, and the ground was mushy. My entire body was slick with sweat, and my long curly hair stuck like a stamp to my head. I thought I was going to pass out.

We were walking through a sweltering tropical climate where old people regularly keeled over and died from the heat, where the poorest of the poor lived in makeshift shacks and were never seen until after dark. Here, summer is a beast that will melt a person alive and leave the remains for the gators.

The roadside we were walking was narrow and covered in seashells, which made a terrible crunch and caused my feet to wobble. My farmer's brogans with their steel-tip toes were the wrong kind of boots for hiking. Excruciating, nickel-sized blisters rose on the sides of my toes, and my socks were spotted with blood from a growing collection of raw, oozing sores. With every step, my feet felt as though they were ripping apart. I had no idea it would be this hard. I wasn't prepared.

My new husband, Peter, and I were wild-eyed newlyweds committed to walking 3,000 miles across America and writing about our journey for *National Geographic* magazine. Still on the first leg, we were crossing southern Louisiana's deep Cajun swamp country in the Atchafalaya Basin, near the Gulf Coast. It was the thick of July, and the conditions were ripe for a python to slither out from the overgrowth. Even though I grew up in the Ozarks, I still shrank at the sight of a snake. Every crackle and hiss from the swamp made me jump.

By the time we met, Peter had already walked from New York to New Orleans. I was in seminary, pursuing a master's in religious education. I loved ancient history, reading philosophy, and meditating about God and things of a spiritual nature, but seminary became a corset for me. I was being squeezed into religious conformity. What I really wanted, though I dared not say it above a whisper in my buttoned-up, buckled-down world of future preachers and future preacher's wives, was excitement. I had a true longing for it. Then Peter arrived on campus.

The Yankee from Connecticut was walking across America, or so people said. Our campus was a spot for him to rest and write about his travels along the way. He was jaded after Vietnam and searching for America's soul. He showed up one evening at a party with wonder in his eyes. I was intrigued. You could tell from miles away that he was a free spirit. I saw something in his scruffy red beard and sun-worn skin that I recognized in myself. I guess he saw it, too, because we ended up spending all our free time together, falling deeply and desperately in love.

Eight months later, it was time for him to go back on the road, and he invited me to come with him.

Out of shock, I laughed in his face.

I wasn't cut out for sports or athletic ventures, let alone walking all the way to the Pacific Ocean. I had the physical fortitude of a kitten and the stubbornness of an Ozarks' mule. I told him it would take an act of God to convince me. I prayed for one in earnest. So did Peter.

Before he left, I agreed to attend church with Peter one last time. There was a guest preacher, a tiny, wheelchair-bound woman named Mom Beall, whom I didn't think much of at the time. Then they pushed her up to the pulpit and she told the story of Sarah and Abraham, the couple who did the impossible. Next, with steel in her eyes and honey on her tongue, she announced the title of her sermon: "Will You Go with This Man?"

We got our miracle. It was the kind of sign that makes cynics into believers, that makes a woman on her own path step into the unknown.

Five months later, we married and left New Orleans on foot, headed toward Texas and, eventually, the great Pacific Northwest. We guessed the journey would take us two or three years.

———

To walk across America in 1976 was revolutionary, foolishly romantic, downright crazy. Only seven years earlier, *Apollo 11* had landed on the surface of the moon and Neil Armstrong had declared "That's one small step for man, one giant leap for mankind." People no longer traveled by foot, in covered wagons, or on horses. Although both of my grandmothers traveled in covered wagons as children in the late 1800s, I was a pioneer by bloodline only. I didn't like being blistered, smelly, or unclean in any fashion. I was not a beach babe, sun worshipper, mountain woman, gardener, or anything close to an outdoors woman. I had never camped a day in my life. As a child in the Ozarks, my nickname was Prissy because I didn't get dirty like the other girls, not even when I played in a mud puddle. Only a week in, I was convinced the walk was not for me.

As we trudged through Cajun country, the Louisiana heat felt like a sample of hell, a taste of the eternal torture to come. Everything I had taken for granted was gone—no house, no air conditioning, no bed, no bath, no toilet, no regular meals. My body was melting like butter. Peter marched on with purpose.

It had been a long, cruel day in the lowlands, and the sun was inching down to the horizon. For safety reasons, we searched for a campsite at dusk so no one could find us. We were harmless, just a young couple hiking, but people traveling cross-country had ended up murdered for less. Peter was an imposing figure, and I was cautious by nature. By being vigilant and careful, we thought we had nothing to fear.

Long shadows fell across the road, and I became acutely aware of my tired, bloodied feet. I shifted the weight on my shoulders, a state-of-the-art aluminum-framed backpack (by a new company called Jansport) bulging with supplies: a sleeping mat, sleeping bag, clothes, water bottle, snacks, first aid kit, personal supplies, tennis shoes, notebooks, a Nikon camera, and a few rolls of film tucked close to my trusty New Testament. With everything packed tight, it weighed almost forty pounds; Peter's weighed twice as much. Our greatest protection, I thought, as we slugged through the southern snake-infested state, was the fact that we looked like humpbacked humanoid monsters.

Just as we were about to slip into the woods to set up camp for the night, an old, mud-covered, beat-up sedan drove slowly past us. Chills ran up and down my spine. We picked up our pace and walked farther down the road, not wanting the driver to see where we entered the woods. Suddenly, the headlights moved back toward us. The car drove slowly around the bend, turned, and came back at us for a third time.

We sensed danger. In these parts, there were folks you didn't want to mess with. Some people in the low country were superstitious and practiced black magic and voodoo with chicken bones, dolls, candles, and skulls. We'd heard stories about innocent people being kidnapped and murdered and never found because they were hexed, tortured, killed, dumped in the swamp, buried in quicksand, or eaten by alligators. The Louisiana police used the Napoleonic Code from the 1800s, and we weren't certain the sheriff or his deputies were prepared to combat the powers of Darkness. As the lights shone closer, Peter and I jumped off the road and scrambled into a soggy grove of tall pines and dead trees. We stood perfectly still, scared little rabbits about twenty feet off the road, hardly a breath between us. We had to wait until it was dark before we could pitch our tent to be certain the old car and suspicious driver were long gone. We stayed quiet and patient.

Looking through the spindly pines for the better part of an hour, we watched him creep by a final time. Maybe he was just curious about hikers in his neck of the swamp. Maybe he wanted to put a little spell on us. Or throw us to the gators just for fun. My imagination went into overdrive.

Finally, we had enough light from the moon to settle in the underbrush. We kept extremely quiet as we staked the tent, moving our hands quickly, soon crawling inside the two-man dome. We zipped the door shut and laid our exhausted, tense bodies on the foam mats, listening to the lullaby of a hoot owl crying and tree frogs croaking.

Before I finally fell asleep, I heard things splash in the bayou and some dead limbs break. I could've sworn there were footsteps in the distance. Our tent gave the illusion that we were safe, but it was just that. An illusion. I prayed to God we wouldn't meet any of the water moccasins, wolves, witches, or alligators on the other side of the nylon walls. I wondered if Peter was as scared as I was, but when I looked over, he was sleeping like a great old bear through winter.

The woods were dark, damp, and sticky when we woke around sunrise. It was early in the day to feel relief, but that's how I felt. At least we'd made it through the night without a swamp creature eating us or the creepy man in the beat-up sedan coming by for another visit. We rolled up our mats, took down the tent, loaded our gear, and strapped on our backpacks. My body shrank an inch when the pack settled on my shoulders. It felt like the weight of the world, and it was going to be tied to me for the next fifteen or twenty miles.

Birds chirped, squirrels bounced, and all the creatures we couldn't see stirred as we stomped through the forest floor and back toward the road. Suddenly, I started to itch. I assumed it was from chiggers or bug bites. Maybe it was the sting of my own sweat or swamp mosquitoes. Or maybe it was poison ivy because it was everywhere. The itching spread over my entire body, and it was getting worse and worse by the moment.

When we pushed through the last wall of bushes and reached the road, I looked down and saw that my arms and legs were covered in masses of tiny specks that looked like dirt spots. I tried to brush them off, but they stuck like glue. I took a closer look and realized that it wasn't dirt at all, but a mass of seed ticks.

I screamed to the high heavens, threw off my backpack, jumped up and down with my arms waving every which way, trying to brush off the bloodsucking arachnids. There had to be a million of the tiny devils sucking on me. Somewhere in the brush around our campsite, I got tick-bombed; fortunately for Peter, he escaped the attack.

For the rest of that day and many thereafter, I pulled seed ticks out of my hair, from my waist, armpits, groin, legs, and ankles, and with each foul bite, I asked God why. The walk was only just beginning. I considered quitting with every bloodsucking tick I pulled off but remembered Mom Beall's sermon and the moment I had said yes to this journey. I believed her words were the sign I had been praying for. I was meant to go with Peter, to be here in this repulsive swamp with ticks under my fingernails. But it was hard—very hard—and I hated it. I was not muscular, too pale and too soft for the elements. And I had a very bad attitude.

Unlike Peter, I wasn't out to make history. I was just a poor, prissy hillbilly girl from South Eleventh Street who grew up on the wrong side of the tracks, who didn't know which direction the sun rose or set.

TWO

SOUTH ELEVENTH STREET

Poplar Bluff, Missouri, 1955–1958

Next to the railroad tracks was a gravel road lined with shabby houses: South Eleventh Street. I called it home. Most of the folks on South Eleventh were illiterate, hardworking descendants of European immigrants from Ireland, England, Poland, and Germany. Everyone received government commodities of canned pork, butter, dry beans, and bags of flour, and meager assistance checks.

At the entrance of our dirt driveway stood a giant oak tree that I'd played under as far back as I can remember, and each old house, including ours, had an outhouse. When you walked down the street, you'd see front porches littered with swings, dumpy sofas, and metal chairs. Every yard was cluttered with ranks of wood, rusted cars, plows, sheet metal, and trash. Some people had chickens that roosted in the junk and squawked at the wandering hounds, who were pregnant, flea-bitten, and eaten up with mange. Those cluttered front porches were where we'd find our neighbors telling stories and idling away the hot summer evenings. Old men would spit tobacco in the yard, and women would chew when no one was looking.

Our four-room wood-frame house was the nicest on the street because it had a screened-in front porch. When he was home, Daddy cut our lawn with a push mower while Mother planted rose and lilac bushes, lily of the valley, butterfly shrubs, and flowering apple and pear trees. The blooms were a cheerful, welcome color against the rust and trash that surrounded us. Our home at 2022 South Eleventh cost $5,000, and I'm sure my parents made payments as long as we lived there.

On the edge of the Ozark Mountains, in the southeast corner of Missouri, my hometown was built on the backbone of railroads, and agriculture. With cotton and rice fields to the south, Poplar Bluff, a hub for the Missouri Pacific Railroad, was a rugged town full of beer joints and railroad workers who drifted from job to job.

We had the largest switchyards outside of Kansas City and St. Louis and a prominent red-light district that stayed open until dawn. Behind the half-acre garden plot where we planted tomatoes, corn, potatoes, and green beans were seven lines that led to the switchyard a mile away. Every day we heard engines chugging and iron wheels screeching. The locomotives were loud, but their sounds were as common to me as birds chirping or dogs barking. All my childhood was spent watching trains and listening to the whistles of locomotives. On summer nights, I fell asleep to the hum of a fan in my bedroom window and, off in the distance, the familiar, mournful wail of a train whistle. It was like a lullaby, long and low. As the train rumbled near our house, sounds of metal on metal shook the earth until it passed. The clackety-clack of wheels lulled me to sleep and was better than a ticking clock. When a train roared by, our whole house shook, and my imagination lit up and went wild. I wondered where everything and everyone was headed.

Quite often when I was older—about ten or so—Mother would send me on foot to Cotton Baker's grocery store on Highway 53 to buy three pounds of ground beef (for less than one dollar), and the shortest route was across the tracks. I crawled under boxcars, climbed over couplings, and squeezed between trains to get to the other side, careful to avoid getting grease on my clothes so Mother wouldn't find out I was cutting through. It was illegal and dangerous to crawl under trains. I made sure they were at a complete stop before I hugged the ground and wiggled my way under them, scouting for linemen and engineers along the way. There was a legend that if you walked nine rails without falling off, a lock of hair from your future husband's or wife's head was under the ninth joint of the track. I walked those rails my whole childhood but never could complete nine of them because they were too narrow and slippery. It didn't stop me from trying. Once on the other side, I hoofed through more poor neighborhoods in south Poplar Bluff to Cotton Baker's and then home again. Mother was none the wiser.

Mother had rules, though not in any specific order. If I violated them, she slapped me upside the head.

- Cleanliness is next to godliness. Keep the floors swept and mopped.
- Look presentable, and don't wear wrinkled, soured, or dirty clothes in public.

- Pick up your shit. Hang up your clothes because that is what a closet is for.
- No trash or junk in the yard or we'll look like our poor, white-trash neighbors.
- Don't track mud in the house.
- Wash yourself every night. Mother didn't like women or girls who smelled "pissy."
- Wash your face and brush your hair and teeth.
- Look alive.
- Wipe your ass.

"It ain't no sin to be poor, but it is to be dirty!" Mother said. "Have some pride in yourself."

I had a knot lodged in my throat most of my childhood because I believed my life would end if I uttered a word at the wrong time. Mother was fiery and angry for reasons I didn't understand. I never knew day to day, hour to hour, what to expect from her and spent most summer afternoons at a distance, lying in the grass and watching clouds float by. They reminded me of people, animals, houses, mountains, and magical places. I was full of fantasies about the world beyond Poplar Bluff. Daydreams took me far away from my neighborhood, the poverty, and our hillbilly kin, though Mother didn't like me dreaming much more than she liked me getting dirty.

Before we had an indoor bathroom, us kids bathed in a #2 galvanized washtub, the same tub used on wash day. Mother would set the tub on the kitchen floor and pour in kettles of hot water until the basin was full up to our ribs and just the right temperature. Jimmy, Vicky, and I had to take a bath at least once a week, and all of us used the same water. When it was my turn, I yelled for Jimmy to cover his eyes and not peek. I sat naked and cross-legged and played with a bar of Ivory soap that turned the bath water to milky gray. Ivory soap never sank; it was like magic. I used to imagine it was a raft and I was Huckleberry Finn.

"Ya little shit, get yer head out of them clouds, or I'll knock some sense into ya!" Mother warned.

But it didn't stop me. In my mind I was always headed somewhere, ears open for the sound of the train, eyes open to the sky, longing for a river raft and great adventures to call my own.

THREE

BAPTISM OF THE ROAD

Westlake, Louisiana, Fall 1976

B eing on the road was not at all what I imagined. It felt like we had been walking for months, yet we were still in Louisiana. The journey across America was a far cry from my romantic daydreams and girlish fantasies. The truth is that walking fifteen miles a day in sweltering heat with heavy backpacks, and as newlyweds, was torturous, inhuman, and degrading. It was a baptism of humiliation. Each mile created new blisters on my feet, which were intolerable when they popped and bled. Our route was along old Highway 90 through the heart of Louisiana Cajun country and away from major interstates. It was desolate, and the humidity was relentless. We hunted for dry ground to camp each night and prayed we weren't struck by lightning during one of the daily thunderstorms.

One afternoon, as we moved like tired laborers in a cotton field, we noticed a layer of storm clouds gathering overhead and heard a rumble in the distance. Storms appeared out of nowhere across the Deep South and on a regular basis. Soon, rain droplets splattered our hats and sunglasses. We needed to find shelter fast. More people were killed each year by lightning than by tornadoes or hurricanes. Within seconds, it started to pour, and we knew we were in trouble.

Up ahead, we saw an open shed on the side of the road and hurried to reach it. Thunder boomed, and in seconds, lightning bolted across the sky. Rain pelted our bodies and made it hard to see. Peter sprinted ahead while I lagged behind. I knew it wasn't safe to be in the open, but it was impossible for me to move any faster with so much weight on my back. Eventually, I joined Peter, and we huddled together under the shed's metal roof, barely protected.

This wasn't like traveling by car. We couldn't pull off the road and wait in safety for a storm to pass. We were exposed and vulnerable. We heard a loud explosion as a brilliant white light flashed, and electrical sparks sprayed like Fourth of July fireworks. An angry jag of lightning fried a telephone pole less than ten feet from us; this was my first brush with nature's fury. When the rain died, the telephone pole sizzled like a scorched matchstick. Instead of resting and processing our first near-death experience of the journey, we picked up our stuff and kept walking. Neither of us had anything to say; we were speechless that we had escaped being fried.

I was the tortoise; Peter was the hare. He walked ahead and turned around often to wait on me, frustration and impatience written on his face. This was not an idyllic way to start married life. Rather than softening, my brogans were getting worse somehow, turning my feet into festering stumps. I walked at a slower pace to manage the pain, preserve energy, and keep momentum. I had to.

"You're as slow as a ninety-year-old woman!" Peter shouted.

"My feet hurt, and I'm walking as fast as I can!" I yelled. "Go ahead, leave me behind!"

The arguing continued in spurts and wasted the stores of energy I had left. Peter claimed I was putting on an act and could win an Academy Award. When I finally hobbled next to him, he grabbed my arm and told me to pick up the pace because we had to make it to the next town before dark. He gritted his teeth.

"Get your hands off me," I said through my own gritted teeth.

"Will you hurry up?" Peter's face was as red as his beard. He gripped my arm tighter while I fought loose and slapped his face. A car honked as it went by. Peter clamped his hands on my shoulders and pushed me backward, just hard enough to cause me to trip and fall to the ground. I was enraged and embarrassed. I cried hot tears as I picked up a handful of gravel and threw it at him as hard as I could.

"Hitler!" I screamed. "You're worse than a dictator!"

Peter threw his hands up in the air and asked God why he was being tortured with such a stubborn, hardheaded woman for a wife. I knew he had a temper and spouted off without thinking, while my anger simmered and was a slow burn. Back in seminary, when I asked if he needed help with the draft of his first article for *National Geographic*, every mark I made turned into an argument, and each page became a battleground that ended in a kiss. Back then, we would yell and bicker, but by the end fall into each other's arms.

On the road, things were different. It wasn't a steamy runaway romance anymore. Fights erupted daily because of fatigue and the differences in our physical abilities. Peter was broad shouldered, rugged, and strong, and I wasn't. He knew the rigors of the road, and I was learning. But I was tenacious and stubborn and hated to be a quitter. And I really hated being ordered around. My mother had done that my whole life. I wasn't going to have it. I was determined to prove that I could keep going.

We were a few days out of Westlake, Louisiana, when we stayed with Preacher and Bobbie Hebert, the kind and generous parents of Wally, a friend and doctoral student from seminary. Mr. and Mrs. Hebert offered us shelter from the heat, a clean bed and bath, plus a once-in-a-lifetime experience in the swamp. Preacher was a blue-blooded Cajun who knew the bayou like a blind person knows braille. He could find his way through hidden coves and meander tangled marshes and dark watery paths anywhere in the Atchafalaya Basin.

Early one morning, Preacher and a relative, Glenn Hebert, planned to head six miles into the swamp to check their alligator traps. They asked Peter to come along but didn't invite me. Their unspoken code: women weren't allowed to hunt or go to the swamp camp. It was a "man thing." I was excited when Peter suggested it would be good for his next article if I could join, and I quietly savored being the first female allowed to trap alligators with the wetland warriors. I had learned that men were territorial and didn't want women around when they bonded with their buddies, hunting, drinking, playing poker, or hanging out. I was glad to sit quietly at the rear of the boat and take it in.

The mud boat was wide and flat and glided easily through miles of marsh, lily pads, and salt grass. A hazy mist hung over the murky water as we inched toward a grassy bank. Preacher had to check one of the lines, which was nothing more than a thick rope dropped in the water with a dead blackbird on the end of a large hook. When Preacher reached for the rope, it jerked and almost yanked him right into the water. Something big tugged on the other end. The men pulled and heaved as the boat tilted from side to side and nearly flipped over in the brown water. I sat still on my bench seat and held my breath.

Everyone yelled as a huge, knotty head emerged. A giant gator opened his jaws, showing what looked like two feet of sharp teeth. He growled with the fierceness of a lion and fought violently. His enormous tail, the size of a log, swung back and forth and banged against the side of the boat. I hung on for dear life. The men shouted at each other that he was a five-hundred-pounder while water spouted up as if from Old Faithful. A typical American gator grows to be eleven to thirteen feet long and could weigh eight hundred pounds; this one was maybe fifteen feet long and probably weighed a thousand. The men said he had to be about fifty years old. The creature thrashed in the water as the men, with one final pull, raised the gator's dangerous head out of the water.

Then Glenn aimed his gun. A loud crack echoed across the swamp when he shot the gator between the eyes. The sound of gunfire faded into silence, and our feelings of elation were mingled with awe and sadness as we watched the old king of the swamp die. The men worked frantically to hoist the heavy, prehistoric-looking beast into the boat. He had to be tagged. It was the law to have permits to bag alligators, and the Heberts had 114, one for each trap. With human population growth and urban development, culling the number of alligators was important. They were aggressive predators. Anything that moved was their prey, and everyone had a story about a child or animal snatched by one of the reptiles and dragged underwater to its death. Before the day ended, we trapped six gators. As we made our way through salty breezes and a soft light back to camp, I stared at the animals, stacked like filets in the mud boat.

I was a whole world away from the days of being college Yearbook Queen, dancing all night with Peter in the French Quarter, and bantering over theology at the seminary. The men dealt with the hefty carcasses at camp while I stared out at the bayou and wiped a film of sweat and swamp from my forehead. Though my body was sore and my mind was tired, something flickered deep inside me—like a spark from a campfire that had come alive.

In an earlier century, my grandparents traveled in covered wagons across Kentucky, Missouri, and Arkansas in search of a better life and land to homestead. They owned almost nothing and endured every hardship imaginable. I wondered if their true grit might be in my blood. Did their determination run through *my* veins? They had risked everything to find new ground and settle untamed places, working the land from sunup to sundown. They believed sweat equity would reward them. Would my farmer grandparents be insulted that I whined about the heat, blisters, and discomforts of walking across America? Would they tolerate my softness and my diva attitude? Somewhere in my DNA, I must've had the wherewithal to do a hell of a lot more than I thought I could. If it were in me, I had to find it.

We pushed on through Louisiana to where the bayou dried up and turned into Texas.

Four

DICK

Poplar Bluff, Missouri, 1949

FOUR

DITCH

Poplar Bluff, Missouri, 1959

D own the road and around the bend from our house on South Eleventh Street was Pike Creek, a narrow, stagnant, and toxic waterway with snakes and rats and a playground for the boys. We called it the "Ditch" because it was nasty and nothing more than an overgrown slough. When my brother, Jimmy, was ten years old, he liked to hunt for minnows and crawfish in the Ditch. That summer he was hospitalized with ringworm, picked up from playing barefoot in the filthy water. He nearly died, and after the infection, Jimmy was stunted and never grew into a tall or strong man. Mother said "that nasty ditch and all its ringworms" damaged his heart and health. Secretly, she blamed Daddy most because he wasn't around to take Jimmy to fish in a clean lake.

South Eleventh Street was in the poorest, lowest-lying section of Poplar Bluff, and when heavy rains came, Pike Creek rose and covered the road. In fact, much of south Poplar Bluff flooded every year; more than once, the smelly water crept up into our house.

Mother was always furious because it wrecked the linoleum in the kitchen, warped the floors, and damaged our furniture. Everything we owned was secondhand or from an auction, but furniture was hard to come by for people like us. Sometimes, if the water got high enough, we'd evacuate in boats after dark when it stopped raining.

The summer I was eleven, the flood came and left water so deep you could paddle around in a jon boat. I wanted to go out with Jimmy and a neighbor boy, Mike Ross, but my brother didn't want me in his boat or anywhere in sight. He said girls were not allowed, especially his stupid sister.

I begged and pleaded with Mother to let me go with the boys, so she told Jimmy to allow me in the boat. I was shocked that she let me do it, but it was one way to get me out of her way. Jimmy frowned when I climbed in and told me to keep my mouth shut.

If I were going to ride in his boat, I had to be quiet and paddle. I did as I was told. Jimmy and Mike laughed and jostled the boat back and forth to scare me while I tried to move the oars. They hoped I would reconsider and get out, or at least they pretended they did. Mike was a sweet boy, and I knew he had a crush on me; I liked him too. I wanted to show off, to prove I could do anything he and my brother could do, so I continued dragging the oars through the slimy brown water.

"Paddle harder!" Jimmy said. "Go this way, stupid! Turn around!" The boys howled and made fun of me.

I didn't like being laughed at or intimidated. I felt my blood heat up and my cheeks turn red. My fingers tightened around the handles, and I sliced through the sludge like it was nothing. Jimmy rocked the boat again.

Enough was enough. I took the paddle and swung it at Jimmy, but he dodged and leaned to one side. His quick retreat caused the boat to tip, and before I knew what had happened, I fell over and splashed into the nasty brown flood water from Pike Creek; it was a real hillbilly christening. I went straight into the sewage from everyone's outhouse. The water was only waist deep, but I came up swinging, screaming, spitting slop, and swearing I would get even.

I hated Pike Creek, and at that moment, I would have given anything to throw those boys overboard too.

FIVE

TEXAS HEAT

"The Breaks," Texas, Summer 1977

We looked bizarre. More like extraterrestrials from outer space with giant golfing umbrellas attached to our backpacks for protection from the scorching sun. We were so odd-looking that small-town newspapers sent reporters to interview us along the side of the road to find out why a young man and woman in outdoor gear would walk across the Lone Star State in one-hundred-degree weather. Gawkers figured we were on some kind of assignment, maybe missionaries or part of a government operation; our state-of-the-art equipment made us look official. Passersby honked and gave us curious looks. Texans couldn't decide if we were aliens, hitchhikers, drug dealers, or worse, but they knew we had a purpose. And they sure wanted to know what it was.

I was learning to ignore the stares and gossip as we walked through one dusty Texas town after another, the same roads where cattle and horses crossed. In Seymour, a shiny Lincoln Continental stopped next to us at a street corner. Inside the car sat five older ladies with coiffed hair, painted fingernails, and heavy makeup. As soon as the car stopped, the women's mouths dropped open as they locked their doors. Maybe they thought we were dangerous drifters or wondered how a woman could allow herself to look like me. Dirty. Unkempt. Parched. They didn't know I had not always looked like this. Peter and I kept walking.

Down the road we found a cheap motel. A rush of cold air and the smell of stale cigarette smoke greeted us before we unstrapped our gear and dropped everything on the floor. I was glad we found a place on the edge of town. Somewhere with air conditioning. The carpeting and furniture were from the 1950s. I slumped onto the sagging bed. Peter knew I couldn't walk another step, so he said he'd go find food. He flipped on the television and locked the door behind him. I sat in a stupor as loud, gaudy commercials played.

On the way to the shower, I hobbled by a mirror and didn't recognize my reflection. The person in the mirror was filthy with blank eyes and matted, stringy hair, and she had blotches of sunburned skin peeling off her face, lips, and arms. Just as I looked in the mirror, the Miss World Beauty Contest came on television. One gorgeous girl after another floated in front of judges while I stood half dead, cooked to well-done, in a seedy motel on the edge of nowhere.

I sighed deeply because at this point, I didn't care how I looked. I wasn't out to impress anybody or win anything. Instead, I stepped into a dimly lit, scum-covered shower and stood under a stream of cool, clean water. I was thankful to watch dirt, grime, and sweat go down the drain.

I thought about rising above being a poor hillbilly, becoming a college graduate, studying for a master's degree, walking across

America, and more. Something was happening to me on the road. I was learning to take life one day at a time, one step at a time, and to listen to the natural rhythm of things. I heard the motel door open and close. Peter yelled, "I'm back with food!"

I smiled. I was deliriously happy knowing I was cool and clean and would be eating a juicy hamburger and sleeping in a bed (not on the ground) with the man I loved.

We were west of Fort Worth, headed into a broiling sun and soaked in sweat. It was hot enough to fry an egg on the pavement, and I was hungry enough that I could have eaten fried rattlesnake. We plodded along and came to a shade tree near a Baptist church with a marquee that said, "If You Think It's Hot Here!" We stopped to rest and drink warm water from our water bottles. Peter snapped a picture of me under the sign, and out of nowhere, a sheriff pulled up beside us and rolled down the window.

"What you folks up to?" he asked.

He looked just like Sheriff Buford T. Justice from *Smokey and the Bandit*. He was short and round as a barrel with a cigar in the corner of his mouth and a glint in his eye. He wore a tan uniform and a wide-brimmed hat that, unfortunately, didn't keep his face from becoming greasy with sweat. His half grin was frozen in place. The sheriff was in charge in these parts, and he sure wanted us to know it. Considering the likes of us, he needed information to make sure we were respecting the law and not up to no good in his town. He pulled off his sunglasses and looked me over from the top of my head to the bottom of my boots and then up again.

Peter explained why we were walking in the unbearable Texas heat. Mentioning our work for *National Geographic* was always a lifesaver. Without fail, whenever people heard that we were connected to the magazine, facial expressions changed from suspicion to bewilderment, then to total acceptance—admiration, even. Suddenly, we were viewed as photographers, journalists, and adventurers, not dangerous nutcases or drifters.

The sheriff locked his eyes on my legs and rolled the cigar in his mouth.

"Missy, you got yerself a pair of stout legs," he said. "Why, I'd say you were cornfed!"

He laughed and snorted like a longhorn as gravel flew from beneath the rear tires of his Chevrolet Impala.

He sped away and shouted back at us, "Y'all be careful now, ya hear?"

We told him we would. Talking to strangers meant stopping to rest, even if the conversation was about my stout legs.

Peter grew up in Greenwich, Connecticut, where white-collar workers and professionals took commuter trains into New York City. It made perfect sense why a Yankee like Peter would be curious about country people and old farmers. Americans west of the Hudson River surprised Peter. When weathered ranchers stopped in mud-covered pickups to offer us water, or poor small-town residents invited us to eat at their table or spend the night in their humble homes, Peter was shocked at their generosity. New Englanders didn't ordinarily greet strangers and rarely spoke to anyone they didn't know. He and I were very different, as if we came from different continents—something that would become more apparent with each mile and each little town across America.

Because I grew up in the Missouri Ozarks where we were all down-to-earth and unsophisticated, common people were familiar to me. To Peter, they were damn near exotic. He asked endless questions about their families and lives. He took photographs and listened to their stories. My Yankee husband discovered, to his surprise, that these people were the glue that held our nation together—unpretentious, humble, helpful, and the salt of the earth. And they proved to be a goldmine of information for *National Geographic.* The small-town Americans we met were like the people I had known my entire life. For me, it was normal to help a stranger; in fact, it was expected. Country folk and hillbillies know that sometimes a man can help and sometimes he can't.

One particularly strenuous day in north central Texas, I prayed for a hillbilly man or woman, anyone in a car or truck to come help us. I was physically weak and not sure I could make it to the next town. We dragged ourselves down a lonely stretch of road near Benjamin. We were nothing but tiny dots on the open prairie, baking underneath an enormous sky and a blazing sun. This part of Texas was big and empty. It looked to me like an angry god had hammered the earth into rugged cliffs, red canyons, and eroded washes. It was called "The Breaks," home to mule deer, roadrunners, jack rabbits, wild hogs, rattlesnakes, coyotes, and lots of copper. Occasionally, we saw longhorn cattle on the other side of barbed-wire fences that stretched for miles. We put one foot in front of the other and plodded along, but there was not a thing as far as the eye could see.

By no less than a miracle, we finished fifteen miles and made camp on a plateau, one of the jagged cliffs that overlooked scorched prairies. We pitched our tent at dusk and watched the sun paint swaths of yellow, orange, red, blue, and pink across the sky before slipping away with quiet majesty. It was spectacular. There were no people, buildings, trees, noise, or pollution to disturb the breathtaking close of the day. In the middle of nowhere, it was just Peter, me, and the sunset. It was no honeymoon—I had second-degree burns on my face, arms, and legs, and my lips were cracked and bleeding—but after hundreds of miles, this was another time I felt grateful to set up camp and share quiet moments together. We never said a word as we looked out at the vista.

By twilight, we crawled inside the tent and as soon as our bodies hit the mats, we fell asleep under the darkest sky and brightest stars. Peter usually covered the tent with a waterproof rain fly, but we decided it wasn't necessary because there hadn't been a cloud in the sky. All we wanted was to cool down, lie down, and go to sleep.

Sometime in the middle of the night we were awakened by peals of thunder that shook the earth. The noise was as loud as sonic booms. Rolls of thunder rumbled and roared and exploded. *Ba boom. Ba. Boom.* Then jags of lightning blazed across the sky. *Ba Boom.* More flashes. The extreme heat caused a violent clash in the atmosphere, and heavy droplets of rain pummeled our tent. Ranchers knew that the louder the thunder, the closer the lightning. This thunder was so loud it made my ears ring. This was the kind of supercell that drove cattlemen to root cellars. Only fools like us were outside—and perched on a high plateau. We were sitting ducks.

Bolts of electrical energy hotter than the sun radiated right above our tent, which was staked with metal poles. Rain soaked through the nylon walls, and we were lying in water. We were lightning rods. The storm had grown into an electrical, pyrotechnic display with explosions and flashes of lightning every few seconds. It was an all-out war above us. The wind whistled and blew the walls of our tent sideways. We could do nothing but lie still, soaked to the bone, and pray. My teeth chattered, and my heart raced while Peter tried to be brave for both of us. He never wanted to show weakness or that he was scared of anything. I guessed it was a male ego thing. My body jolted with every loud boom. I was so terrified that I tried to remember Bible verses under my breath. "The angel of the Lord encamps around those who fear him, and he delivers them" (Psalm 34:7 NIV).

We took off our wedding rings and moved everything metal away from our bodies while we huddled together in a pool of water on our mats, contorted in each other's arms, realizing we might actually die. Buzzards would eat us before anyone found our remains. No one would ever know what happened.

It was close to dawn when I woke up. We were still alive, still together.

SIX

THE MINEFIELD ON
SOUTH ELEVENTH STREET

Poplar Bluff, Missouri, 1959

"You hard-headed little shit! You ain't got a lick of sense!"
I had no idea what I had done wrong this time and wanted
to run out the back door.

"You better listen to me, or I'll slap the livin' hell out of you!"
Mother yelled.

Her tirades erupted often and took me by surprise. They
seemed to get worse over the years, instead of better. When I asked
what was wrong, or if I dared counter her, she turned on me like a
cornered cat.

"Don't you talk back to me!" she went on. "I'll take a two-by-
four and knock you up b'side that silly head!"

Although we lived next door to Granny and Granddad, who
were my old angels, life was a minefield under my roof. Mother

exploded in a rage over the smallest annoyance, which usually had something to do with me.

One time a neighbor girl, Sue, came to visit. I offered her a cookie and a glass of milk. We were talking and laughing when Mother entered the kitchen with a scowl on her face. I could see she was angry, but I didn't know why. Mother told Sue to go home because I had chores to do. As soon as she was out the door, Mother turned on me with vengeance.

"My God! Don't you know we can't afford to feed the neighborhood?" she seethed. "You don't have the sense God gave a goose. You're as thick as a brick wall!"

I was paralyzed and confused but didn't dare open my mouth. How many times had I witnessed Mother feed dirty hobos? She was generous enough to share leftover white beans, cold fried potatoes, and day-old cornbread with every drifter who darkened our door and even sent them on their way with a peanut butter sandwich and an apple in a brown paper bag. I watched her read mail to the Schwitzers, the Larsens, and the Lipscombs because she was the only one on the street who could read. She helped our neighbors, and in return, they gave us homemade cakes and cookies. Poor old Mrs. Schwitzer made the best oatmeal-lace cookies with water because she didn't have oil or milk.

Why did Mother help everyone and yet I wasn't allowed to offer a cookie or a glass of milk? Why was she so angry? Why was she so angry at me?

It was baffling.

When I was old enough to connect a few dots, I figured Mother must've been spoiled as a child because she was the baby of her family and her brothers catered to her. Now, nobody was spoiling her. Daddy worked all the time, and she had to raise us kids by herself. That was my best guess, and all I had were my childish conclusions. There were no answers because no one talked, but I knew she wasn't happy.

Betty Jo Crain, my mother, had been stunningly beautiful as a girl, with long, curly auburn hair that glistened in the sunshine. She had greenish hazel eyes, a wide smile, and a feisty streak, and country boys fawned over her because even though she could have been a beauty queen, she was a tomboy, ready to play games, throw rocks, swim in the creeks, climb trees, and take on the world. She had a spark.

With a house full of brothers after her only sister died of pneumonia, Betty Jo was placed on a pedestal. She was the diva of the family, especially after she developed rickets due to improper food and lack of vitamin D. She walked to Poe School in Oxly, Missouri, with other hillbilly kids and graduated from the eighth grade. She was smart, extremely creative, and quick-witted, but she hated academics and never wanted to attend high school. Instead, she wanted to paint, write poetry, arrange flowers, play music, sew, quilt, bake, and do just about anything besides sit in a classroom.

She ran free in the country and later wrote about her happy childhood to her mother, my Granny, after paying a visit to her old homeplace.

Dear Mama,

I went home today, back to the old place where, as a child, I had many carefree, happy, barefoot days as well as cold winter nights snuggled in the featherbeds upstairs in that old log house.

The hand-dug well, lined with native stone and the big rambling cabbage rose beside it, offered a cool drink. The gazebo-type shed over it is in bad disrepair, but I could still see you, Mama, in my mind's eye drawing water there.

The big oak trees that I used to climb, play around, and swing under are still there, extending long arms for other children's games.

Mama, the old house is long gone, but the cedar tree you and brother Glenn planted out back is a big thick haven for birds to nest in springtime, sing their songs in summer, and find shelter in the cold snowy winter.

Hollyhocks overgrown with weeds nodded their colorful heads as I walked by to the old apple tree just outside the yard where, on a warm moonlit summer night, the mockingbird sang his many songs that would float away on the breeze.

Oh Mama, if you could have just walked to the pond with me, up the dusty lane with the wildflowers and grasses on either side. How I wished for you, Mama, to sit with me on the bank, pitch pebbles in the water, watch the ripples ring out; you would tell me about the wild plants and how to use them, care for, and love them. Our outdoor walks were always a learning experience; you knew so much.

We could have watched the dragonflies flit and dip over the water, a butterfly sit on my shoulder. Mama, you would always say, "You will get a new dress that color."

The good times, the bad times we had on the old home place. The years and many, many loved ones are gone, but the memories and the love are still there.

Yes Mama, I went home today, to the old home place, "But only in my dreams."

Betty (Crain) Pennell

Youth was a fairytale that lasted just seventeen years for Mother. One afternoon, she and her girlfriends strolled Main Street in Doniphan, Missouri, an Ozarks hamlet on the banks of Current River, when she noticed a young man leaning against a storefront. He had one foot braced against the wall, and he wore blue pants and a white shirt. He was tall and thin with thick, curly black hair and very good-looking. When Betty Jo walked by, he winked at her.

On that day, she and her girlfriends made a pact: "Marry a good-lookin' man, even if he ain't worth a damn!"

Six months later, that's just what she did. She married Ernest Pennell, that "good-lookin'" man from Doniphan, in the courthouse in Poplar Bluff. It was 1943. She wasn't yet eighteen, but she lied about her age to get hitched.

The newlyweds stayed on the Pennell homestead for half a year without worries or responsibilities, churning ice cream, roasting peanuts, playing music, swimming in Current River, and dancing at the state line on Wednesday and Saturday nights. They were easy, fun-filled months. But before long, the couple had to pack up and move to St. Louis to work and save money.

Within a year they saved enough to pay cash for a country store and operated it together until my brother, Jimmy, was born. Daddy wasn't there. He wasn't there when I was born either. Mother said she almost died because of that old "quack" doctor in the sketchy brick building off Main Street in Doniphan. She never forgave Daddy for not being present then or afterward. He couldn't make a living running the country store in the middle of nowhere, so he went to work as a mechanic in the city.

Mother was alone. And she was mad about it.

SEVEN

BELLE IN A BONNET

Crowell, Texas, August 1977

Old-fashioned telephone lines buzzed across West Texas with news about the couple hiking across the Lone Star State *and* the unexpected death of Elvis Presley. It was August and hot as hell. Ranchers crowded in local cafés to gossip and drink coffee. They talked about cattle rustlers, fence posts, and barbed wire, about who shot the biggest rattlesnake and who had seen a wild hog, and they asked, "Where are those crazy hikers now?"

"Yes, sir-ee, I saw them near the Wichita River."

"They're damn fools to be walkin' in this heat."

"The paper says they're fixin' tuh write somethin' for the *National Geographic*."

"Well, hope they ain't bit off more than they can chew."

"Damn fools, they are!"

We were walking toward Crowell, Texas, in the furnace-like heat one afternoon when an older couple stopped to offer us water. They pulled up in a new, white, air-conditioned pickup with a big cauldron of water in the back. Everyone in a radius of 100 miles knew who we were because Peter and I had been featured on the front page of local newspapers, and every rancher kept an eye out for us to see if he could help.

"Howdy," Homer Martin said as he stepped out of his pickup. He towered six feet tall and wore a wide-brimmed cowboy hat.

"We figured y'all might like a cold drink."

He invited us to rest inside the cab of his truck, and I nearly fainted when I felt the rush of cold air. It wasn't long before Homer and his wife, Ruby, welcomed us back to their ranch for supper.

"We live about five miles east of here in a wide spot called Gilliland," Homer said. "It's nice to live out in the country 'cause if I take a notion to whip Ruby, nobody can 'ear her a-hollerin'."

Ruby laughed and told her husband to be quiet. It was obvious Homer adored his wife and had teased her for nearly half a century.

They were in their midsixties and lived in a modest three-room ranch-style house they had built in the 1940s. It was one level, low to the ground, and surrounded by 320 acres of wheat and cotton fields. The Martins were considered dry-land ranchers and farmers because there were no rivers, creeks, springs, or ponds. Rainfall was all they had to nourish the soil. Rows of cotton grew within a few feet of the front porch; you could reach right out and grab it. A yard with grass was a waste of good water to dry-land farmers and ranchers.

A few battered and stunted trees leaned to one side and grudgingly offered shade. We saw clothes on a clothesline flap in the wind, and chickens scratched in bare dirt next to a root cellar. The area around the house was littered with old plow blades, pitchforks, a 1949 tractor, 1954 pickup truck, and piles of junk that became home to rattlesnakes, jackrabbits, and coyotes. I heard something rustle.

"Only kind of animals I don't take to is corals, cottonmouths, and rattlesnakes," Ruby said. "Law-w-w, girl, I've killed hundreds of them things. Just killed a big rattlesnake last week. Knew he was in there, and I was waitin' fer him to come out."

Ruby stood straight at five-foot-eight, 150 pounds, and carried herself with pride. She always wore a bonnet to protect her eyes from the Texas sun. The creases in her face were as deep as canyons, and her blue-gray eyes were narrow from a lifetime of squinting. Her hair was short and gray, and she wore it in a 1920s style with waves pressed against her head. She wasn't much of a talker, but her eyes danced when I asked her questions. She told tales about moving to Texas in a covered wagon and how she raised her twelve brothers and sisters. Now I understood why she never wanted children of her own.

She and Homer married in 1933 and first lived in a one-room shack. They herded cattle, shot jackrabbits, picked cotton, and survived as best they could. They started out with apple crates for furniture, and the boards in the shack had cracks as wide as her thumb. They poked old newspapers and rags between the gaps to stop snow and rain in the winter and tried to keep warm with a wood heater. Ruby didn't have trouble remembering where she and Homer started their married life. She could see the old shack they lived in from her back porch.

"Most folks like to ferget their hard years, but I like seein' how far I've come," she shrugged, staring out at it.

Supper turned into a few days of rest. After soapy baths and a couple nights of sleeping in a bed instead of on the ground, I felt rested. We enjoyed giant portions of Ruby's home cooking, which was simple, hearty, and always topped off with sweet tea. I could have stayed forever, but Peter was itching to get back on the road. On our last day with Homer and Ruby, Peter pulled out a map of the United States to show Homer our potential route. I forced a smile. I had to. Looking at the map was a sucker punch.

After a year of walking, we were only in west Texas. The entire western United States, from Texas to Oregon, looked overwhelming and impossible to me. We might as well have been traveling from the earth to the moon, on foot, one step at a time. Dear God, I'd already been through swamps, ticks, alligators, bleeding blisters, dehydration, and almost being struck by lightning. I swallowed my reaction but wished I could scream, run away, or say *shit* like my Mother did, and say it real loud. I wanted to quit. Again.

Ruby saw the look on my face and interrupted, sensing I was disturbed. She quickly asked if I wanted to check the cattle with her.

Yes, I thought. *Anything to get out of here.*

We jumped in the ol' pickup and drove to a corral where they kept a small herd of black angus. The cattle were Ruby's children, and she checked on them herself every afternoon before dark.

The sun started to sink as I hung over the fence rails and watched Ruby weave in and out of the herd. The cattle bawled and shoved against each other as they sauntered to a water trough. The windmill made a half circle in the hot evening breeze while a pencil-sized stream of water flowed into a trough. Ruby pushed her way to her Beefmaster bull, who refused to move any farther. He was a heavy beast of 2,000 pounds, and he was angry. He hedged Ruby against the fence. I thought for sure she was a goner.

Skilled and unafraid, Ruby lifted a mesquite branch and popped the bull with a quick snap. When the massive animal felt the thorns on the switch, he lowered his head and pawed the ground, facing her. He snorted, and dust flew around his nostrils. His beady black eyes glared at Ruby.

"I told you to move," she said. "When I say to move, I mean for you to move!"

The bull swished his tail defiantly and stepped toward her with his legs apart. I held my breath. I knew the bull was going to charge, but Ruby didn't budge. She popped the switch again, so hard it cracked and echoed across the corral. My heart was in my throat. Boy was I glad to be on the other side of the fence.

Ruby yelled at the bull once more, "Now, mister, I said to *move!*"

The bull snorted and pawed the ground with his hoof. He took a step toward her. With an iron tone she yelled, "I ain't movin', 'cause I *cover* the ground I stand on!"

The old gray-haired woman in a bonnet wasn't afraid of this bull, rattlesnakes, coyotes, or anything that walked or crawled. The bull tossed his head back and forth as he glared at his owner, who stood stock-still. To my surprise he backed up. The massive animal slowly turned around and lumbered in the direction Ruby wanted him to go. He was like an overgrown teenage boy who knew better than to face off with his mother.

When we arrived back at the ranch house, Peter and Homer were on the front porch. They were glad to see us pull up, because dark, rolling clouds loomed in the distance where the earth met the sky. Storms were a regular occurrence this time of year, and after camping on the plateau in The Breaks, Peter and I were better acquainted with them than we'd like to be. We sat on the porch and watched the sky to see what was going to happen.

Dusk settled and a wall of dark clouds lined the horizon, just near the back of Homer and Ruby's wheat fields. Suddenly, buckets of rain arrived, pounding the metal roof on the porch. A headwind blew Homer's cowboy hat off, and the temperature dropped swiftly. Rain blew sideways, and we were wet before we made it inside the house. I watched the window curtains flap over the kitchen sink from strong gusts and felt my heart quicken. I looked for the slightest sign of fear or anxiety from Homer or Ruby, but there was none. They were alert and stoic. It started to hail.

The lights in the house flickered for a few moments and then went out. The four of us watched from inside the front door, and sure enough, when the sky lit up there was a black funnel in the distance, hanging from thick clouds, spinning like a giant, twisted rope.

"Yes, sir, it's probably hittin' Vernon right now," Homer guessed.

Vernon was a small town northeast of the ranch. Homer and Ruby were storm watchers, and they knew when to run for safety, but for now, we watched nature's assault on their neighbors. We saw and heard buildings collapse in the distance, windows explode, roofs being ripped off, and trees uprooted. We were right in the middle of Tornado Alley. People who weren't in cellars or a safe place were likely sucked up and carried into the night.

"You gotta respect nature in these parts," Ruby shrugged. Texas wasn't a badland to her; it was just cantankerous, and you needed to learn its moods.

We stood in a tense silence, watching and listening to the roar of the tornado as it moved across the horizon like a runaway train. Peter and I were holding our breath, ready to run to the root cellar on command. With a burst of lightning, the black clouds were beginning to scatter. The funnel had turned north and was moving away from us.

We gave a collective sigh. The electricity flickered and came back on. Homer and Ruby seemed confident danger had passed and acted like nothing had happened. It was just another day on the ranch. Ruby rushed to the kitchen to prepare supper. The clatter of plates and silverware comforted me as we ate at their little Formica table under a picture on the wall of The Last Supper.

Peter and Homer were in a serious discussion about rattlesnakes when I asked for the last piece of cornbread. Ruby lifted the plate to pass it, but Peter grabbed the cornbread without thinking. Ruby slapped his hand and gave the last piece to me. "You bet!" she said. Peter laughed and said, "Oops!"

After Ruby and I washed and dried the dishes, the men kept talking, and we moved to the front porch to sit and rest. Everything was quiet, like the earth had taken a good bath and it was time for bed. A lone coyote yelped in the distance, and a canopy of stars twinkled overhead. The sky was desperately clear. We sat in silence and smelled the fresh-turned dirt, sagebrush, and weeds that had been uprooted by the tornado.

I preferred to sit in silence, but Ruby wanted to talk, for once, about our walk across America. She knew I was troubled when I had looked at the road map earlier, and she wanted to question me about it. I tried to sound upbeat and brave, but she knew something was wrong. I could feel her eyes pierce me in the dark.

Reluctantly, I admitted I was exhausted and hinted that my marriage was not what it appeared. To walk across America was truly an adventure, but the physical challenges—the aches, pains, blisters, thirst, and hunger—never stopped. Hesitantly, I confessed to Ruby that Peter pushed too hard each day and accused me of pretending to be in pain. I even told her I'd called him Hitler.

I swallowed my tears and readied myself for the sympathy of my new friend. Ruby knew the truth now, that our marriage wasn't perfect, Peter was demanding and insensitive, and I was tired.

She waited a few minutes before speaking.

"I know this is hard," she reasoned, "and it ain't easy walkin' 'cross this country, but yer doin' somethin' bigger than yerself."

I was shocked. Hell, I knew I was doing something bigger than myself! I wanted pity! Advice!

"Law-w-w-wd, girl!" Ruby went on. "You ain't lived 'til you've picked cotton all day long in the hot Texas sun fer 25 cents a hundred pounds. Draggin' that sack, yer hands bleedin', yer back breakin', boilin' up, and not makin' enough money to buy groceries."

Ruby wasn't being hard on me. She saw my situation through a different lens. She was a living, breathing pioneer, a plainswoman who had traveled from Oklahoma to Texas in a covered wagon in 1915. She was not soft. She grew up unbelievably poor with a dozen siblings surviving on gravy made with water, not milk. At sixty-five, she'd lived through starvation, she'd chopped and picked cotton, planted and harvested wheat, and worked as hard as any man in Texas. She and Homer weathered the Great Depression in a shack. She wasn't impressed with my attitude or my fancy hiking gear.

"Law-w-w-wd, girl!" she said again, shaking her head. "This walkin' across America . . . well, now, it ain't nothin'! Come on. Girl, you can do this!"

We talked quietly as crickets serenaded us. Ruby never spoke against Peter, and she didn't sympathize with me. Instead, she dared me, challenged me to keep going, to be my own person, to learn what I was capable of. Ruby was courage in the flesh, a messenger from another generation. She assured me that I had everything I needed to walk to the Pacific Ocean. I wanted to believe her as her words hung like stars in the Texas night.

So I kept on walking.

EIGHT

HILLBILLY ANGELS

Poplar Bluff, Missouri, 1960

G ranny and Granddad lived in a gray, brick-sided shack next door to me, and I thought they were old angels with arthritis who were hard of hearing. They were Mother's parents, and they loved to dote on Jimmy, Vicky, me, and their twenty-three other grandchildren who came to visit from time to time. There was a well-worn dirt path between our houses that couldn't grow a blade of grass in spring if it tried. I saw them every single day of my childhood.

Grandad swore the world was going to hell in a handbasket because young people didn't pick cotton, plow, or work in the fields. They had too much time on their hands and spent all of it dancing to *American Bandstand* and listening to rock 'n' roll on transistor radios and had their noses stuck in front of black-and-white televisions.

"These youngins' need to learn how to work 'cause idle hands are the devil's workshop!" he said as he spit tobacco.

When Jimmy was twelve years old, Granddad complained that my brother needed to work in the fields, and because I was younger, he said I could hoe and plant seeds in the garden. Vicky didn't have to do anything, Granddad said, because she was too little and not good for much at all yet.

Granny was a tiny, plump woman. She was kindhearted and soft-spoken, and I never saw her wear anything besides a cotton dress and an apron to keep her dress clean. She always wore a homemade bonnet whenever she worked outside and never wore lipstick, mascara, or any kind of makeup. Her long, gray hair was almost always pulled back into a bun, and because women from her generation didn't wear pants or show their bare legs, she wore cotton stockings all year round.

"Beauty is only skin deep," she always said. I wished she would stop saying that to me because I didn't understand what she meant. After all, Granny was exotic-looking, with soft dark eyes and delicate features. When she was a girl, her hair was thick, black, and fell to her waist. She never took credit for her beauty or even seemed to notice it. She claimed her great-grandmother was Cherokee and had passed on her high cheekbones and mild temperament.

I spent many long, sweet, and fanciful hours with my Granny, and because she lived next door, I often stayed overnight in her homemade featherbed that had a chamber pot underneath it. She snuggled next to me in bed, and before we said goodnight, she'd pinch my feet with her wiry toes to show affection. She snored like a racehorse, and Grandad did the same in the bed next to us. I loved staying with them, but between their snorts and bubbles it was hard for me to fall asleep. When I discovered Granny dipped snuff in secret, I assumed it got stuck in her mouth and nose and was the cause of her snoring.

On Friday nights, we ate popcorn and watched *Rawhide* and *Gunsmoke* on their portable TV. If we didn't watch television, she told me stories.

"Please, Granny, tell me what it was like when you were my age, back in the olden days," I'd say.

She never mentioned the pain in her knotted fingers or how her hands shook from palsy when she brushed my hair. In fact, my Granny never complained about anything. She didn't have an ounce of self-pity about being dirt-poor, cooking on a wood stove all her life, not having indoor plumbing, and even now, living in a shack with thin plastic curtains over the windows.

Their shack next door to us was all Granny and Granddad had to show for a lifetime of farming and hard labor in the Ozarks. Granny never considered herself a victim of anything or anyone because she saw in everything the joy of living, even though she had outlived three of her children. I was too young to understand Granny's life or her heartaches. She didn't question or swear against President Franklin Roosevelt when her sons fought in World War II. She didn't raise her fist at God when death, droughts, and starvation knocked at their door. Granny had a connection to heaven and earth and didn't waste her breath cursing God or humans each time weather or hunger forced her family to move. She had endured and absorbed great sorrows, absorbing them like roots soaked up the rain. She never complained, never yelled. She was nothing like Mother; only once in my life do I remember her raising her voice at me.

I was just a kid, around seven years old. Granny and Grandad were still living in Oxly, Missouri, a tiny Ozark town of one hundred people. I stayed a few weeks with them over the summer and met a new friend one day. We played in Granny's yard for a while, and then the little girl asked me to walk home with her.

Distance meant nothing to me, and I was excited to go to my friend's house. We skipped, giggled, and threw rocks down a lonely gravel road and as a child, I thought we were a long way from Granny's house and the village.

Before I knew it, the sun began to set, and it was getting dark. We had walked over a mile when I heard Granny yelling my name. I turned around and saw her speed-walking toward me with a green switch in her hand. I had never seen such an angry look on Granny's face.

"Where on earth have you been?" she asked. "I've been looking everywhere for you!"

I didn't understand why she was so upset and worried. I explained that my playmate invited me to her house, but Granny wouldn't hear it. She was "mad as a wet hen."

"There's wolves out here! You're too little to be walkin' anybody home!" she said.

As soon as we reached my friend's house, Granny turned me around and switched the back of my legs all the way home. I cried and explained I didn't know the girl lived so far away and that I wasn't lost. Granny didn't care. She went on about the wolves and switched me some more. I bawled as loud as a newborn calf. Crying, I told her, "I'm not afraid of wolves!"

———————

That was the only time I ever saw Granny angry, and it was because I walked too far from home—a harbinger of my life to come.

NINE

ROCKY MOUNTAINS AHEAD

Sangre de Cristo Mountains, New Mexico, September 1977

Texas was finally behind us, and since my talk with Ruby, I felt inspired to keep on walking. We moved slowly away from tornadoes, longhorn cattle, and deserts, from the scorching wind and black oil fields of the Panhandle, and entered New Mexico with promises of cooler temperatures and mountains ahead. We were in the northeastern corner of the state, progressing like turtles on the prairie. We'd been on the road for sixteen months.

The landscape was wide open, hot, and windy. We were nowhere upon nowhere, but we pushed ahead with the tumbleweeds, spending six days and nights between towns and eating a lot of peanut butter sandwiches. We drank out of windmills and camped in waist-high golden grass. After crossing the border, even though we were moving slowly, both of us felt more energized, excited to be walking across new terrain. We were bolder and much stronger since we'd left New Orleans, but there were days we snapped at each other because of fatigue, hunger, and sore muscles, and I lagged farther behind because I was angry.

Whenever we argued, Peter said I was pathetic and called me names. I had been called names my whole life, and I countered that he was a monster. I didn't know what to do or how to fix our marriage from the shoulder of a lonely two-lane road. I planted one foot in front of the other as I looked down. It was easier to carry my heavy backpack when I tilted forward and kept my head down. Peter was a quarter mile ahead of me.

Suddenly, I heard something off to the side. I turned my head to look, and there were two young pronghorn antelope, a male and female. They stood on the other side of a thin wire fence and stared at me. They cocked their heads and blinked. To them, I was misplaced and clearly didn't belong in their habitat.

I forgot the weight of my pack and lifted my head. Beyond the fence line were entire herds of them, a band off to the left and another to the right. They were everywhere, as far as I could see, roaming and playing. Their slender, deer-like bodies stood about four feet tall with reddish brown markings and white belly, rump, chest, and cheeks. They had real horns, not antlers. I was amazed at their beauty and wanted to pet them.

"Oh, give me a home where the buffalo roam and the deer and the antelope play," I sang in my head, watching them amuse themselves and play freely with each other.

The animals stared at me with their dark, protruding eyes as I stepped carefully toward the fence. They were only yards away when a group of them shot up into the air and ran fast; it was like a shockwave. I didn't know it then, but antelope are the fastest animals in the Western Hemisphere. They can run sixty miles per hour with bounds up to twenty feet, and they can detect movement four miles away. But my curious little pair on the other side of the fence stayed close to me. Their eyes were locked on mine, and we all tried to decide who was wild and who wasn't. We fascinated each other.

I walked along the fence row, ever so slowly, and watched from the corner of my eye as they chased each other. Peter waited for me to catch up with him, and as we walked along, the antelope did too.

When we stopped, they stopped. I cooed and told them how beautiful they were. We strolled together for three enchanted and unforgettable miles. I admired their unity and prayed Peter and I would reach an equally harmonious relationship. They tilted their heads and seemed to smile like inquisitive children. Did they like us? Did they feel safe?

Out of nowhere, their rump hairs stood on end. Maybe it was a change in the wind or they sensed danger, but they jumped straight up and bounded toward Apache Canyon. I smiled behind them, watching until their bodies disappeared. Did these darlings really join us on our walk across America?

That experience reminded me of John Muir, the famous naturalist who said it best, "All that the sun shines on is beautiful, so long as it is wild."

———————————

Gradually, the desert transitioned into the Sangre de Cristo Mountains as we rose slowly in elevation through Cimarron Pass on Highway 64. A Spanish explorer discovered the mountains in 1719 and named them Sangre de Cristo ("Blood of Christ") because the red and pink hues on snowy peaks reminded him of the crucifixion of Christ. They were the southernmost subrange of the Rocky Mountains, which stretched north to Alaska for three thousand miles.

When I finally laid my weary eyes on those mountains, I understood the way pioneers felt when they first saw the peaks. They had traveled in covered wagons, on foot and horseback for hundreds or thousands of miles across rivers, plains, prairies, and deserts, through all kinds of weather and were drained from hardships and attacks from outlaws and American Indians. For every traveler who survived, the Rocky Mountains became the doorway to heaven. My feelings were an emotional stew: numb, thrilled, relieved, shocked, overjoyed, and mostly grateful to have reached what felt like the Promised Land. A sense of great accomplishment filled me.

Inside the white peaks before us were waterfalls, blue rivers, and green and fertile valleys. The Rockies offered shelter from heat, dust storms, tornados, and poisonous snakes. There were trees and grasses, high pastures for livestock, and heart-stopping beauty. I was too excited to consider anything beyond cooler temperatures and shady forests of green, but in truth, the Rocky Mountains were deadly too. They held extreme blizzards, avalanches, wolves, bears, and no food. The elevation would also be challenging. The muscles in my body ached from crossing the prairies, so how in God's name was I going to make it where the air was too thin to breathe and the steep bedrock was meant for bighorn sheep, not human beings? Squinting at the peaks, laid out like a row of alligator teeth,

I thought of Ruby Martin and my Granny. I reminded myself that pioneers didn't stop because of setbacks or dangers. I had walked from below sea level in New Orleans to over six thousand feet. I would do this, too, and hoped my marriage survived the peaks and valleys ahead.

We were walking toward Eagle Nest, New Mexico, when I dropped my Nikon camera on a narrow two-lane road. It rolled into the middle of the highway at the same time a semitruck rounded the curve. Peter and I both froze as our mouths flew open. We didn't agree on plenty of things, but we both understood the pictures on that roll of film in my camera could not be replaced. Everything I had photographed was about to be destroyed. The truck's enormous wheel rolled over the camera that had been my faithful accessory, my friend, all the way from New Orleans, and I moaned in agony deep inside and out. Aside from the fact that I loved the Nikon, I needed it, and it would take weeks before a replacement from *National Geographic* reached us in some town up ahead. We would have to calculate how many days it would take to reach a phone, then find a post office in the next town or the town after that to pick it up. The loss was devastating. My entire body shook as I waited for the truck to pass so I could properly assess the damage.

I grabbed the Nikon from the road and found a dent on the thirty-five-millimeter lens, but nothing else. I examined it from front to back and back to front. I tried to advance the film. I held it nervously and was shocked to snap another picture. We both released deep sighs and I shouted, "Thank You, Lord!" The old girl still worked. I imagined her clinging to the pictures I had taken of cottonwood trees, variegated cliffs, and perfect pairs of antelope as the shadow of the truck moved on down the road. Like they say, "A picture is worth a thousand words," and that roll of film held moments locked in time. The Nikon allowed me to take pictures for three thousand miles (some of which would end up as full-page spreads in the August 1979 issue of *National Geographic*).

"Let's go," Peter said, staring ahead and calculating how many miles we needed to walk before we camped for the night. His body grew smaller and smaller against the rugged landscape. I embraced my Nikon like an old friend and captured another picture of Peter with a click. The muted light was perfect.

TEN

GRINGOS AND OUTLAWS

San Luis, Colorado, September 1977

We had an hour before sundown as we trekked northwest on Highway 159 in southeastern Colorado. It was another hot and strenuous day as we headed toward San Luis, the oldest occupied town in Colorado. There was nothing as far as the eye could see; the narrow strip of blacktop ahead disappeared over the horizon. No cars. No houses. Nothing but sagebrush and a fiery sun that would disappear shortly. The knowledge that we were crossing a lawless territory began to sink in.

In this region Catholic churches were the most prominent buildings. You would see them, without fail, sitting in the center of every small town, surrounded by clusters of adobe houses. The priest's messages of peace and goodwill should have been for everyone, but gringos like us were not included. We had been warned to be careful, told we were traveling on foot through unfriendly country. New Mexico and southern Colorado were populated with descendants of Spanish Conquistadors who deeply disliked foreigners, especially gringos. To this day, they considered the area as their land and not part of the United States.

———————

Peter and I were from back East; we were naive to the history and culture in the area. Before crossing state lines, we had been given a series of warnings by the locals that in this part of the country the class structure was different:

> The Pope (Roman Catholic)
> Spanish Americans
> Mexicans
> Navajos
> Apaches
> Utes
> Black Americans
> Gringos (Peter and me)
> Texans
> Satan

We were just a notch above the devil. I wasn't sure how true any of the class structure was, but that didn't stop me from wanting to get out of the San Luis Valley as quickly as possible.

Peter walked a good distance ahead of me as I watched a red-tailed hawk swoop over the sagebrush in search of small prey. The close of the day was normally my favorite time. The sky was filled with the sweet warbles of robins, ravens, doves, and goldfinches before they found refuge for the night. The wind grew still. Off to the side I saw a handsome jackrabbit hop through the brush, and I smiled a little sadly. I felt moody and quiet.

I'd entered the Rockies feeling hopeful, thinking that if I kept walking, if I focused on moving forward, things would get better. Our arguments had grown worse. I wanted peace and understanding between us. We didn't know how to talk to each other, and neither of us had much energy to try. I couldn't figure out what I had done to irritate Peter or why he was so critical of me. I asked myself over and over what was wrong.

Most newlyweds started marriage with romantic dinners, music, and wine, making love several times a day in a comfortable bed under soft sheets. Our possibilities for romance were about the same as going to the Sahara Desert. We were human pot roasts, baking eight hours per day in extreme heat, then heading to bed on the ground, on top of rocks and cow patties, under bridges, on plateaus, wherever we could camp safely. And I was dirty. I smelled bad and hurt from head to toe. Nothing about my body or appearance was sexy. Nothing about me wanted to be touched. Rest and safety, not sex, was on my mind in this lawless territory. It frustrated Peter, and he was angry.

He was sharp-tongued and demanding, even after fifteen miles of walking. When he tried to pull me next to him inside the tent, I told him we both smelled like shit and I was too tired. He felt rejected and called me "prude," "iceberg," and "fanatic." He told me religion ruined me and that I needed to loosen up. In so many ways, from New Orleans to New Mexico, I had given everything I had, every ounce of my energy and part of my body. The personal attacks hurt, and his lack of sensitivity left me dumbfounded, but I tried to overlook his tirades. I needed to save my energy for the rigors of the walk. Peter's short fuse was no secret, and I hoped everything would be fine once we lived in a house and slept in real beds, once both of us were clean, rested, smelling good, and ready to be together.

The sun became heavy as I walked and prayed for our relationship. Then I heard a motor off in the distance. Sounds carried for miles across the open range, and I assumed the vehicle was far away. The entire day we had only seen a couple cars on the desolate highway, but within minutes, a rusted, greenish-gray, two-door Plymouth sedan rumbled and slowed down next to me. The car was jacked up and shook as it rolled to a near stop. Peter was nearly a quarter mile ahead. He stopped, turned around, squared his shoulders, and hurried back. My heart raced as I walked with my head down. The car crept beside me, and I tried to hide how nervous I felt. Nothing like this had ever happened before.

From the corner of my eye, I saw the man behind the wheel. He was straight out of a John Wayne western, with long, thick, straight, blue-black hair and a red bandanna around his forehead, and his dark eyes were glassy with blood pockets in the corners. He held a beer bottle in one hand and steered the car with the other. His brown skin was greasy and sweat dripped down his cheekbones and jaw. Two other men were seated behind him.

"Hey, señorita," the driver slurred. His voice was slippery with venom. "Want a ride, señorita?" The car engine was rough and pulsated as the men laughed and coaxed me to get inside.

The driver took a gulp of beer and bounced the car forward, then stopped. The men stretched their arms out of the windows trying to grab me and shouted obscenities I couldn't understand. They were totally drunk. I hopped off the shoulder of the road toward the ditch as they raised beer bottles to offer me a drink, begging me to get in the car. I walked faster and would not look at them.

"Ah, come on, señorita! Get in the car!" they demanded, then laughed.

The car rolled along the shoulder of the highway as the men made foul gestures. I caught my breath as I saw Peter in front of their car with his giant golf umbrella. It looked like a spear. There was no doubt he would whip their asses. The driver cursed, shoved his old car into reverse and ripped it into gear, then floored it straight toward Peter. He was going to run him over.

Peter jumped off the road out of the way, and we both ran into the open sagebrush. The car stopped and backed up, brakes smoking, before it barreled into the sagebrush after us. The driver screamed and cursed and seemed hell-bent on running us over. Dust rose like a storm cloud when the car turned in circles, bounced back on the road, and came to a stop. The largest of the three got out and stumbled toward Peter with a knife. He swore and slashed the knife through the air, but he was so drunk that he staggered and nearly fell. He then retreated to the safety of the car.

At that moment, we heard a truck in the distance, and a pair of headlights came into view. It was almost dark. Thank God another vehicle was in sight. It might as well have been the cavalry because it felt like we were going to be saved. When the drunk men saw the headlights, the driver peeled out and his tires squealed. He screamed back at me as they sped away.

"We're coming back to k-e-e-l you!" His threat echoed across the silent desert. "We're going to k-e-e-l you, señorita!"

They were serious. I was sure of it.

As they drove down the road Peter and I raced like scared rabbits across the brush into the open desert until we found a sunken gully surrounded by tall brush. We hunkered down and waited until the moon was the only light, just like we had in the bayou. We couldn't risk being discovered. It was too dangerous to pitch our tent, so we quietly unrolled our sleeping mats to sleep under the stars and prayed we weren't on top of a den of rattlesnakes. We peeked through the shrubs and watched the road as the moon climbed higher in the sky. Sure enough, the men returned, driving fifteen miles per hour up and down the lonely highway and promising they would find us.

They shone a flashlight across the desert for nearly an hour, and sometimes the light lingered in our direction. Eventually, they gave up and disappeared on the empty highway and back into the night.

We took a deep breath and thanked God for our safety, at least for now, and waited another thirty minutes to make sure they were gone before uttering a single word.

"Do you think they would have killed us?" Peter asked. He expected me to cry. Part of me wanted to, but Mother's fire surged through my veins.

"Are you kidding?" I laughed. "Humph! I was going to take on the littlest one!"

I looked at my husband in the moonlight and loved him, admired him. I was too tired to tell him that he was my hero, but I snuggled close and whispered, "I love you" as I closed my eyes.

We slept very little that night and gathered our gear before dawn, scurrying five miles into the town of San Luis, population 781. We walked as fast as we could straight to the sheriff's office to report what had happened.

"Those boys are part of a gang out of the Culebra Mountains," the sheriff said. "They kill people for the fun of it." Clearly, they were old news to him.

The sheriff's report jolted me. This stuff really happened and it was for real.

"Yup," he sighed. "That gang tried to kill me, too, until I threatened to blow out the leader's heart with a sawed-off shotgun. The San Luis Valley's worse than the Wild West now."

He held up a sawed-off shotgun like it was the only thing that made a difference.

"They don't give a damn for the law, and you guys are lucky to be alive!"

That night, the sheriff allowed us to pitch our tent on the back lawn of the courthouse.

ELEVEN

ERNIE'S MOTORWAY

Poplar Bluff, Missouri, 1960–1965

D addy was next to God because he was the same person every hour of every day. Unflappable. I adored him. Not once did he raise his voice at me, not even when he caught me smoking one of the neighborhood boy's Lucky Strike cigarettes, the unfiltered ones that were strong enough to choke a burly sailor much less a young girl of thirteen who didn't understand the consequences.

Daddy put out the cigarette and said he didn't want me to smoke. Breaking Ernest Edward Pennell's heart was worse than breaking my own. One look from him, and I knew I had fallen from grace.

"Do you think I'm bad?" I asked him.

"No, you are not bad!" he chuckled, trying to hide his broad grin.

That single intervention kept me from smoking until I was a freshman in college.

Daddy was tall and thin with hazel eyes and thick, black, wavy hair. He was very handsome. As she promised, Mother got herself a good-lookin' man. Plus, Daddy was well-read. He wasn't like the hillbillies on our street; he subscribed to *National Geographic* and *Arizona Highways*, lots of travel magazines, and the daily newspaper. He also loved reading car and mechanic magazines to keep up on trends.

———

Daddy worked long hours at Ernie's Motorway, his truck stop, and by the time he got home each evening, he was exhausted and too tired to engage in family matters. In those days, men were expected to be the breadwinners and heads of their households. Hillbillies looked down on men who didn't work hard to provide for their families, and one time I overheard Mother talking about a relative who was shiftless and wouldn't provide for his kids.

"Why, that lazy son-of-a-bitch ought to be horse-whipped and thrown in jail!" she said.

———

Daddy wasn't around much, but he was hardworking. She respected that.

During my early childhood in the 1950s, the entire country was focused on the American dream. Especially in the Ozarks. Because millions couldn't find work and went hungry during the Great Depression and World War II, people were determined to better themselves as the economy rebounded. Even hillbillies didn't want to live on rations, be sent to the poor house, or go hungry again. Daddy was no exception. It was time to get off the farm and move to the city, own a house, buy a car, and have modern conveniences. Get stuff. Buy stuff. Own stuff. Hoard stuff. Get more and more. Daddy swore he would never return to the backbreaking farm labor he knew as a boy, and he never did. Instead, he worked pumping gas, washing windshields, changing tires, and repairing engines and trucks.

As a boy, Daddy was exceptionally bright in math, reading, mechanics, and music, and he skipped several grades. He attended Cyclone School, a one-room building in Harris Township. When he completed the eighth grade, his parents didn't have money to send him to high school, so he worked on their fruit farm to help the family survive the Great Depression.

Ernest Pennell continued to learn as he worked on the farm, tinkering with anything mechanical. Before long, he repaired, rebuilt, and made all kinds of engines hum. No engine was too difficult—tractors, cars, lawn mowers, semitrucks, anything with gears. With his aptitude, he became an expert mechanic and eventually bought his own truck stop on Highway 67 in Poplar Bluff and called it Ernie's Motorway. This Mobil Oil filling station and truck stop with a café stayed open 24–7. The sign—a neon flying red horse visible for miles—would go on to be a sought-after antique.

Daddy had an agreement with Strickland Trucking Company to dispatch truck drivers, and Ernie's Motorway became a terminal and lodging with bunks and showers. His business prospered and became a hub for hillbillies, truckers, mechanics, farmers, and men who wanted to congregate around a cup of coffee. To me, it seemed like the most exciting place in the world.

I wasn't allowed to spend time at the truck stop or café because it was dirty and greasy and filled with roughneck truck drivers. They were called "road cowboys," hard-living men who drank whisky at night and nursed headaches over black coffee and scrambled eggs before getting back on the road. They also chased women and told dirty jokes through clouds of cigarette smoke. Truckers liked to play the jukebox and pinball machines and stared too long at young girls and women who walked into the café. I was curious and wanted to go, but neither Daddy nor Mother would allow it.

In seventh grade, I told some kids that my daddy ran a truck stop and was a mechanic. They called him a grease monkey. After that, I was embarrassed to tell anyone I lived on South Eleventh Street or what my father did for a living. Some of the parents of my classmates were professionals like nurses, doctors, pharmacists, and judges, while Daddy and Mother came out of the Ozark hills with eighth-grade educations. It wasn't until I entered junior high school that I realized I lived on the poorest side of town, that I was low class and a *gen-u-wine* hillbilly.

Daddy didn't play baseball in the yard, wrestle with Jimmy, or interact with us kids very much. He seldom talked and was not affectionate or demonstrative. His routine was the same: he worked, ate, slept, and repeated it seven days a week. Fifty-two weeks a year. Mother's routine was the same too: she worked on her art projects and complained about feeling sick or being a slave. She was on edge all the time.

Although he never spoke harsh words or hurt my feelings, I questioned why Daddy wouldn't defend me or stand up for me in front of Mother. He never told her to stop when she called me Essie Drowns.

Essie was a mystery character Mother compared me to daily. I wondered who she was, and it hurt when I found out she was a simple-minded, ignorant hillbilly girl. Mother called me Essie most of my life.

"Essie, get yer head out of them clouds and get them dishes done!" she said. "You wake up in a new world ever day!"

I wanted so badly for Daddy to say something.

Maybe she forbade him from complimenting me? Maybe he was afraid it would cause a fight if he paid me too much attention? Was Mother jealous of *me*? The thought was more satisfying than it probably should have been. My parents were separate mysteries. I didn't understand either of them.

At least Daddy was peaceful. He watched the *CBS Nightly News* with Walter Cronkite in the evenings and read the *Poplar Bluff Daily American Republic* newspaper. Then he ate supper, bathed, and went to bed. If we had a conversation at the dinner table, it was short and about world events. He knew what was happening in politics and international affairs and told us not to believe everything we heard on the news because it was biased. I learned the importance of analytical thinking from him.

Our evenings as a family were brief. Immediately after supper, Mother told me to wash dishes and what to do with leftovers. Jimmy was supposed to help, but we argued over who washed and who dried. He purposely refused to wash the plates clean, so we argued until the dishes were done. Vicky was too little to help. Without fail, while Daddy read, the kitchen would be cleaned, the food scraps thrown across the garden, the trash burned, and the floors swept. Mother would not allow us to act like what she called white trash.

My parents were from different planets—at least that's what I thought. Mother was flamboyant, artistic, and quick-tempered, while poor Daddy was good-looking and dull as a dishrag. She was agitated and biting, and he was reserved and compliant. Betty Jo itched for a good brawl. She needed something Daddy couldn't give her. She barked and bellyached about everything, moaned that she was everyone's maid and claimed she was sick and unhappy, but Daddy never said a word and refused to argue with her.

Still, they were looked up to on South Eleventh Street because they had come up from nothing and made a good life for themselves. My mother and dad were hardworking, honest, and resourceful, and both could read and write. It may not have been the runaway romance from the days they laid eyes on each other when Mother was seventeen, but it was an American dream come true with a house, a car, three kids, green grass, butterfly bushes, and food on the table.

TWELVE

ON TO A GOLD MINER'S TOWN

Lake City, Colorado, October 1977

We were headed northwest on State Highway 149 to a gold miner's town in Colorado, tucked under the peaks of the San Juan Mountains and hidden from the world. Lake City was nestled at eight thousand feet and a hamlet from yesteryear; people had dreamed of settling there, but few found that they could stand it." There was no industry and not many ways to make a living. It was so far off the beaten path that deer and elk roamed the streets, and locals left their doors unlocked and windows open in the summer. In fact, it was the *only* town in Hinsdale County and some of the most remote territory in the lower forty-eight. The county had 1,123 square miles of nothing but mountains and, among them, multiple "fourteeners"—peaks exceeding fourteen thousand feet in elevation.

We needed to reach Lake City before we were caught in a blizzard. We moved slowly along a narrow, winding road that snaked through canyons and along the upper end of the Rio Grande until we reached the historic mining town of Creede. The temperatures were falling below freezing at night, and we had another forty-four miles of mountains to go. It was cold, but we were happy with the daily sunshine, royal blue skies, and fluttering golden aspen leaves. They made each mile feel like we were one step below heaven.

We saw bald eagles, elk, and deer as we rounded hairpin curves without guard rails and hiked close to sheer cliffs that dropped down to swift rivers and deep valleys edged by pine forests. The views were epic, and it was like a dream when we reached Slumgullion Pass at 11,530 feet. We didn't experience altitude sickness because our bodies had adjusted one step at a time. Too many unprepared vacationers flew into Colorado to spend time in the Rockies and ended up sick with excruciating headaches due to lack of oxygen. Some died of heart failure. If you were going to enjoy these high exotic mountains, you had to understand their wild ways and respect them.

On the other side of the Continental Divide we walked down the steepest paved road in Colorado with an incline of 9.4 percent. It made truckers sweat bullets and burn up their brakes. We heard stories of drivers who didn't make the switchbacks and drove over cliffs to their deaths. When we came to a place called Windy Point Scenic Overlook, we stopped to rest and absorb the panorama. As far as we could see were jagged, snow-covered peaks. Before our eyes were Uncompahgre, Wetterhorn, Red Cloud, Handies, and Sunshine Peaks. No matter how spectacular the coverage in *National Geographic*, it would fall short of capturing their surreal beauty. Our eyes could barely believe the majesty, and Lake City waited for us at the bottom.

This part of the trip was different from the hot deserts and grassy plains. It was easier to walk faster and farther in the chilly alpine air. After crossing Louisiana, Texas, and New Mexico, I understood why hikers preferred the mountains. We walked effortlessly down the steep and perilous roads toward Lake City, where we planned to hold over for the winter and write about Peter's first leg of the walk from New York to New Orleans, which would end with a James Robison Crusade, our courtship, and our wedding. The writing wasn't just for *National Geographic*; a publisher in New York called William Morrow had offered us a book deal.

With each step, I dreamed about taking bubble baths, cooking pots of homemade chili, watching television, snow mobiling, sleeping together in a bed, and being in one place for a few months. It was the first time in two summers since we left New Orleans that we would have a place to call our own. I prayed that during our winter layover, without the strain of walking fifteen or twenty miles a day, the sweeter side of our marriage would surface because we truly did love each other.

We were a few miles from town when we rounded a bend on Highway 149 and passed a natural deep blue lake called Lake San Cristobal. Then we crossed a milky cobalt river called the Lake Fork of the Gunnison, fed by snowmelt from the San Juan Mountains. Off to the side, we saw a historic marker and stopped to read it. I had never heard of Alfred Packer, but according to the sign he was a legend in Lake City and across the west.

As the story went, gold fever roared like wildfire when Alfred Packer came to the Rockies in the late 1800s to join a party of gold miners. It was 1874 in the San Juan Mountains when miners staggered into a Ute Indian camp near present-day Montrose. Rather than hold over for spring, Alfred Packer and five underprepared prospectors struck out toward Gunnison and into a violent and deadly winter. Two months later, Packer emerged alone and in fairly good shape. He later confessed to killing one of the men in his party who had gone crazy in the freezing weather. Packer said he killed him in self-defense. To survive the deadly winter, Packer ate the remains of the man he killed and of others who had frozen to death.

He was arrested and tried in Lake City, and a local newspaper quoted the judge who sentenced him:

> "Stand up yah voracious man-eatin' son of a bitch and receive yer sentence. When yah came to Hinsdale County there was seven dimmycrats. But YOU . . . you ate five of 'em! dam yah. I sentence yah t' be hanged by th' neck until yer dead, dead, dead, as a warnin' ag'in reducin' the Dimmycratic population of this county. Packer, you Republican cannibal, I would sentence ya ta hell, but the statutes forbid it."

Packer was cunning and used legal maneuvers to win a new trial in Gunnison, which was in another county. He was released from prison in 1901 and died six years later of a stroke. Alfred Packer became infamous as the Colorado Cannibal.

I was spellbound by the story. And after walking all the way from New Orleans, it was a good reminder: the wild can turn a man from sane to mad. Settling in for a season was going to be good for us. We hiked around the last switchback, and there she was: Lake City, the place we would call home for the next ten months.

Lake City rested in a steep-walled valley. When the town was incorporated in 1873, it teemed with five thousand residents, most of them burly miners who forged their way through mineral-rich mountains and crowded into local saloons. Those were the days when Lake City bustled with whisky-drinkin', gamblin', and pistol-packin' frontiersmen. When we entered the city limits, it was clear the town had dwindled. Now, it was a couple of hard-packed dusty streets lined with century-old Victorian homes and a few quaint historic churches. It reminded me of a western movie set with wooden walkways along the fronts of the Lake City Drug Store, the First National Bank, the Silver Street Saloon, the small medical center, and a handful of gift shops.

A big snowfall blew into town as soon as we arrived, so we holed up in our tiny, rented log cabin on Vickers Dude Ranch, the oldest one of its kind in Colorado. The family had been here since J. W. Vickers rode into town on horseback in 1887 in search of gold.

One of his sons, Perk, inherited the historic ranch. He grew up in the shadow of his daring father and learned to mine for gold and silver, raise cattle, hunt elk and deer, build and rent cabins, blast and carve roads through the mountains, and become an outfitter for hunting trips through the rugged terrain. Anything to survive.

"No question about it, living here is tough, and some people just can't make it," Perk said to us when we wandered in. He was an energetic sixty-five years old, short and stocky with a constant twinkle in his eyes and a quick wit.

"Christ alive," he said and chuckled. "The winters are long—very long!"

I liked that he learned to laugh at the Rockies instead of letting them bury him. I hoped Peter and I would do the same. We had all the modern trappings, but winter would be harsh.

THIRTEEN

BLACK COFFEE AND BACON GREASE

Poplar Bluff, Missouri, 1962

I called him Granddad, and he seemed as old as Methuselah from the Bible. Unlike Granny, who was patient, kind, and had a gentle nature, Walter Napoleon Crain was persnickety, easily annoyed, and cranky all the time. Everyone considered him a "character," which was another way of calling him a one-of-a-kind hillbilly. He was witty and opinionated, spicy—yet a photographer's dream, always standing stone-faced like a statue every time he spit his Cotton Boll Tobacco, which he pulled from his brown, twisted pigtail. He never missed the spittoon. I loved the earthy, rich smell of his chew, but the brown spit was disgusting.

Granddad often argued politics and current events, and he swore the next generation was worthless, that the world was coming to an end. Like Mother, he became irritated for no apparent reason, and I learned to stay out of his way. I figured he was disgruntled because of his stiff, arthritic joints and old age. He complained of rheumatism and hardening of the arteries, probably due to a daily breakfast of fried bacon or sausage, fried eggs, biscuits, and milk gravy, all washed down with thick black coffee boiled in an aluminum percolator until it was dark syrup. To finish off, he soaked his biscuits in bacon grease and sopped up the fat until the dish was clean. He said the grease oiled his joints and was good for him. At the time, I believed it.

Born in Bolivar, Tennessee, in 1879, Granddad completed only the fourth grade. He was a tall, handsome young man with flaming sandy-red hair and penetrating, ice-blue eyes. He loved music and was a gifted bass singer in a choir before marrying Granny in Walnut Ridge, Arkansas, in 1903 at age twenty-four, when Granny was nineteen. There wasn't much time before the first of eight children was born. Their entire marriage was about raising kids, survival, poverty, and hard farm work in the rocky hills of the Ozark Mountains. They were just a bunch of poor hillbillies.

It was nearly impossible to feed ten mouths without money, education, or opportunities, so Granddad had to use physical labor, common sense, and the *Farmer's Almanac* when it came to planting and harvesting crops. He followed the moon and heavenly signs, as well as the aches in his joints, to forecast the weather. He said a crescent moon was a "dripping moon," which meant rain and a good crop. He also had a house full of boys at his disposal whom he ruled like a military commander, and he whipped the tar out of them for the least sign of disobedience or laziness.

Walter Crain never cared about worldly goods or making money except to pay taxes and buy flour, salt, staples, and two chambray shirts and one pair of denim overalls per year. He hoped he'd have enough to help a needy neighbor. Feeding his houseful of kids meant walking behind a team of mules from sunup to sundown. He had no time or energy to covet material things; besides, he didn't care about shiny trinkets or useless stuff, except one time when he bought a new truck to transport his hogs to auction.

One day, after a sale at the livestock barn, he drove his truck to the river to wash the mud and excrement out of the truck bed. Current River was a few blocks from the town square and not far from the barn. There was a gentle slope down to the river, so he turned the truck around and backed down the embankment until the rear tires eased into the water. He parked and climbed in the pickup bed to clean it.

Current River emerged from mountain springs throughout the Ozarks, and the water was crystal clear. It was famous for swirling pools and swift currents, gravel bars, rock ledges, and towering bluffs along the banks. Grandad was busy washing out manure when the rear tires of the truck started to inch out of place. He felt the ground move, and the vehicle slipped gently into the water.

He tried to jump inside the cab to drive out of the water, but before he could get there, a strong undertow pulled the wheels, and it was obvious Grandad was in trouble. The truck shifted to one side and started to slowly drift farther from the bank. The river was so strong it pulled the truck deeper. Granddad was trapped in the back as it slowly floated away. He yelled again and again for help because he couldn't swim and was deathly afraid of water, but no one was within hearing distance. He climbed on top of the cab and hollered until he was hoarse. The truck floated downriver and went under a big tree limb. He grabbed it, held on for dear life, and finally made it back to the bank. His shiny new truck floated into the middle of the river like it was on a magic carpet ride, and he watched in disbelief as it slowly upended and went down like the *Titanic*.

"That's the first and last damn motor vehicle I'll ever own!" he said. And it was.

My entire childhood, I never saw Granddad drive a truck or car, and I wondered if maybe that was where his mean streak came from. (My sister, Vicky, swore it was from the whisky he kept hidden in the chicken feed.)

Granddad and Mother were very much alike, and he was the only person I knew who was brave enough to stand up to her. He frequently complained to her that Jimmy should do more work, and she countered that Jimmy mowed the yard and burned the trash and we didn't live on a farm, so what else was Jimmy supposed to do? When Granddad didn't like something, he spit tobacco extra far. I noticed he spit a lot around Mother.

Mother said his guts were ruptured because he pushed a heavy plow all his life. He had to wear a truss, a semicircle medical support that looked like a pair of headphones clamped around his waist to hold up his private parts. Even with his hernia and complicated equipment, he stood up straight. He was tall and bony, unmovable, like a chiseled statue staked to the ground—except when he hunched over to spit tobacco.

One night Granddad died in his sleep after plowing the garden behind his shack, readying the plot for green beans. He was never hospitalized, never had a stroke, didn't have cancer or a terminal disease—he was just a tired old hillbilly farmer and his heart stopped beating. The old man I grew up beside was an uneducated decent human being whose feet were planted on the ground behind a team of mules long before my feet were planted on the road across America.

For most of human history, survival depended on the rising and setting of the sun and the rhythm of the seasons. Walter Crain tilled hilly country and absorbed nature's patterns, never asking for more than his daily bread. He taught me what it meant for the meek to inherit the earth.

FOURTEEN

WINTER IN A LOG CABIN

Lake City, Colorado,
Winter 1977–1978

The winter of 1977–78 was as cold as the Arctic, and I was thankful to be off the road. We hibernated in a two-room log cabin on the Vickers's ranch, but the cabin was not insulated and never meant for winter habitation. It was impossible to keep it warm when the temperature dropped below zero. We threw chunks of black coal in the fireplace and watched blowing sleet and snow out the window. A propane wall heater kicked on when the temperature inside the cabin dropped below freezing.

Outside, the whiteness was blinding. Low-hanging clouds reduced visibility to less than two feet, and deep mounds of snow piled high around the cabin porch and covered the driveway. Day-long storms buried cars and trapped people inside. Those who dared go out had to take survival gear. We heard about truck drivers who slid into canyons and weren't found for days and people stranded in blizzards who froze to death in their vehicles. That winter, one Lake City resident ran out of gas outside town and started to walk for help. The snowplow found him the next morning frozen to death. Bitter winds and whiteouts were common, and anyone exposed was not likely to survive.

After the fireplace died down at night, steam rose with each breath as we snuggled under layers of wool blankets and sleeping bags. It felt good to go to bed rested and ready to snuggle, but it was hard to overlook Peter's continuing verbal abuse.

Peter pounded out a couple pages a day on an electric typewriter as he wrote about his walk from New York to New Orleans. William Morrow, our publisher in New York, wanted a manuscript completed while we were in Lake City, but Peter didn't want to be bound to a desk. He wanted to be out in the wilderness exploring the high country. On days it wasn't snowing, he preferred trapping coyotes, hunting beaver, and taking photographs rather than sitting in the cabin pecking on the machine. I couldn't understand it. His procrastination frustrated me because I learned growing up that when I was told to do something, by God, I'd better get it done. I was taught to "put your hands to the plow" and keep going until the job was done. I could hear my mother say, "Get yer ass in gear!" Plus, I was worried our financial security was at stake; such an important publisher might not be patient. Peter didn't seem to care as he reluctantly wrote sentences, then paragraphs, then pages about how he grew up in public housing in Greenwich, Connecticut, one of the wealthiest cities in the nation.

———————

Peter's friends had fathers who ran international corporations, while his own dad worked for a manufacturer. Peter's childhood friends lived in mansions with manicured lawns, while his family was crammed in a tiny, government-subsidized apartment with six kids and his parents. The contrast was sharp. Peter was the oldest, and his parents expected him to be a role model to his younger siblings. He was motivated to please his parents, be successful, find himself, sort out family issues, and resolve personal conflicts. He wanted to understand the disparity between social classes and politics and get it together in the era when smoking pot and free love were gospel.

As Peter recalled his upbringing and the reasons for walking across America, he enjoyed writing about the Appalachian Trail, discovering a mountain man in Virginia, his experience living with a black family in North Carolina and on a hippie commune in Tennessee, where he lost his lovable friend and first walking partner, his dog, Cooper. Peter was a living Huck Finn; his stories were captivating and exciting, and they drew me in just like he did. The reality, however, was that every writer's manuscript had rough edges. When I smoothed out a line, rewrote sentences, or edited content, we fought like we had back at the seminary. His resentment grew. Each time I explained how editing would make him look good, he accused me of being controlling. Overbearing. He called me a moron. He said I was stupid. Pathetic. Selfish. In my mind, I just wanted to help. My involvement made him so angry that he dismissed me and called me a fat ass bitch.

"Why don't you move back to the Ozarks with the rest of the losers in your family?" he said.

The subconscious Essie Drowns surfaced, and I was right back on South Eleventh Street, a cowering hillbilly nitwit. Peter had no way of knowing he echoed Mother. How could he understand the emotional dynamics in my family? How could I understand the emotional dynamics in his family? I had no idea what caused him to be explosive toward me, but I did my best to shrug off his words. I made excuses for him because I didn't know what else to do. Was there something about me or the way I behaved that triggered contempt? Maybe he thought I was interfering with *his* adventure? Maybe he thought my edits were personal attacks against him? Then I wondered if Peter had a hang-up with strong, ambitious women. If he did, why and how did he fall in love with one? Whatever the underlying reasons for Peter's reactions, I always circled back around to believing something was wrong with me. *What had I done?*

When Peter called me an idiot, a hick, or stupid, the air went out of my lungs. I shrank as if I had been shot. I didn't have the self-confidence or psychological skills to separate my past from the present. I didn't know how to stand up for myself. On the inside, I was a failure.

My favorite song that winter was "Don't It Make My Brown Eyes Blue" by Crystal Gayle. When I was alone, I cried because things weren't right with Peter and me, and I was at a loss as to how to resolve our differences. To make matters worse, he was furious when he caught me crying.

"You think you're the only one who has feelings?" he scoffed.

I didn't think that. I knew he had unsettled and confused feelings like I did.

"Why can't we discuss our relationship?" I asked.

"Because all you want is to be treated like a queen!"

He slammed the cabin door and left me speechless.

For heaven's sake, even Mr. Rogers gave us permission to talk about our feelings. Some days, I had no idea what lived inside my husband's heart other than anger.

When he wasn't on the defensive, Peter had a poet's soul and was romantic. He brought me wildflowers from the hills, shiny quartz rocks, cacti, and other natural treasures. In front of others, he made a big spectacle that I was his country girl, his Southern belle, his prize. In those moments, his exuberance and sense of wonder were magical; he was the most charismatic man I had ever known, and I would have followed him anywhere. But behind closed doors, the name-calling was killing me.

As we walked mile after mile on the road, our relationship grew more complicated and layered because we were portrayed publicly as a model Christian couple, the sweethearts of adventure. We were featured on front pages of newspapers, and our walk across America became a top story on television stations from New Orleans to Colorado, so I swallowed the darts and played the happy wife. We were all smiles for the camera and in front of others, but inside I churned. I was a fraud. I didn't have the know-how to help myself, rebuff the attacks, or save our marriage.

I told myself as winter winds blew outside the cabin walls, that our flawed relationship was as simple as this: we were two immature and wounded people with unresolved childhood pain

SO LONG AS IT'S WILD

who didn't know how to meet each other's needs. Counseling may have helped—we both came from imperfect families, and there was no reason to blame each other for the baggage we'd inherited—but I wasn't sure Peter would go, even if we found a therapist within a hundred miles. My plan was to pray more, be patient, and bow to whatever Peter wanted. If I could hang in there and do those things, I believed our relationship would work out.

I spent our snowed-in days reading and rereading Scriptures about wives submitting to their husbands, so I swallowed offenses to avoid conflict. This only covered my cowardice. I told myself that with love and devotion we'd be fine. I had a lot to learn, and my piety was a foolish strategy. Meanwhile, we made friends in Lake City, ate in local cafés, drank beer in the Silver Street Saloon, and joined our new community for ice fishing and skating. We had lots of good times when we were with other people, where we could put on a show and be who the public wanted us to be. Peter's quick wit and sense of humor drew a crowd and made him the center of attention. His blue eyes sparkled like Christmas lights every time he told stories from the road, and audiences hung on to his every word like he was the pied piper. In those moments, I was just as captivated. I was proud to be his wife.

FIFTEEN

PILL HILL

Poplar Bluff, Missouri, 1967

G ranny never owned a single glittery thing in her life, but she loved bright colors. In December we had an annual tradition to drive to the nicest neighborhoods in Poplar Bluff to see the Christmas lights. We called the affluent area of town Pill Hill because doctors and lawyers lived there. Mother said they were the upper crust, not hillbillies like us. Pill Hill was a small subdivision with brick homes decorated every holiday season in multicolored lights and real spruce trees from an expensive tree lot that sparkled through picture windows. There were life-sized reindeer, sleighs, Santa Clauses, and nativity scenes on every manicured lawn, and every driveway had fancy sedans. I was struck with awe and envy as we rolled by in our old car. Pill Hill was quiet and clean. There wasn't a railroad track or outdoor toilet in sight. I dreamed of living in a nice house someday and wondered what it would be like to live like the rich folk did.

Granny was like a child. "Oh, ain't the lights purty!" she said.

On South Eleventh Street, our holidays were humble, and every year Mother warned us, "Don't expect much!"

She and Daddy couldn't afford to buy either a real or an artificial Christmas tree, so ours was a scrubby cedar from the woods down the road or a pine sapling from the countryside. Mother always chopped it down herself and used her artistic talents to decorate for the holidays. She soaked the tree with water, then dusted the branches with glue and white flour to make the needles appear covered in snow. When she was finished, the tree looked like it had a coat of fresh powder from top to bottom.

We wove strings of clunky, multicolored lights through the limbs and around the trunk to make it glow like a big-city department store tree and adorned the skinny branches with homemade ornaments, popcorn strings, store-bought glass bulbs, and lots of silver icicles. Mother made a star out of tin foil and perched it on the highest bough. To me, it was as real as the Star of Bethlehem. I was always impressed with her creativity and handiwork. I loved watching her cut and fold the foil so that it lay flat, without a single wrinkle, looking like sterling silver. By the time we used several packages of icicles, we thought our Christmas tree was a masterpiece. It looked like a shiny, cone-shaped roll of aluminum foil with colored lights.

We were thrilled. From a distance, you'd think it came straight from Pill Hill.

Granny celebrated Christmas with us every year during my childhood, and when she was eighty-one years old, I asked her what Christmas was like when she was a girl and begged her to write it down so I could read it like a story. Writing was difficult for her because her crippled hands shook with palsy, but she was glad to do it anyway. She used a lead pencil to scribble her earliest holiday memories. She was six years old and traveling in a covered wagon from Kentucky to Arkansas.

Granny's spelling was in Old English, and some of her words were misspelled, but hillbillies from the Ozarks had their own language, culture, and prejudices. All of this was normal to me.

Scheses [Sketches] *of My Life as a Child,*
By Annie Crain

(Left Leitchfield, Ky Sept 1890 and arrived in Walnut Ridge, Ark, January 1, 1891)

"At the age of six, I, the daughter of Tom and Nellie Watson, left Leitchfield, Grason Co. KY. Dad, Mother, and six of us children all in a covered wagon drawin by two big red and white oxens, Buck and Jerry. They had big, long horns with brass nobs on the end of thire horns.

The first night we didn't have a cover on our wagon, in came a big rain. They put us small children in the wagon covering us with a big quilt. The big boys got into a straw stack close by, and Dad and Mother got under the wagon. That was the way we spent the night.

So we stayed there the next day and night and Mother made a wagon cover and a small tent. Did all the sewing by hand. From then on, Mother and us small children slept in the wagon with the big caresene lantern hung from the wagon bows for warmth while Dad and the boys slept in the tent with a big campfire out in front. If there was snow, they would cut brush, put in the tent, and put a big straw bed on the bush to sleep on.

We had a little cook stove called a "step stove" because it was made like steps. First there was the hearth, then up a step, then up another step. Mother would cook breakfast and supper on it.

We camped a week on Green River at Birk City, Indiana. It was a beautiful sight at night to see the big steamboats all lit up with colored lights and the black folks singing and picking the banjo.

As we came down the Ohio River, there were big pins made of fence rails full of corn ready to load on boats. We had to drive between the pens and the River. The oxens would shove and push each other and I was so scared I cryed. I thought they were going to fall in the River.

Sometimes we would camp two nights in the same place while Mother would do the washing and ironing. (by the way, I still have that old iron). Dad and the boys would go hunting for squirl and rabbits. Sometimes, would get a wild turkey, while us small children played, geathered nuts, and picked sweet gum from the trees. We camped for Christmas, hung our stockings on the wagon bows. We each got a gum drop fish about five inches long with a rubber line on them so they would bounce up and down, and a man came by, gave us some stick candy, and the boys drew a big picture of Santa Clause on the wagon. So we had a wonderful Christmas.

We crossed the Miss [Mississippi] River at the Cape in a big ferry boat. There was a cabin in the middle of the boat for pasengers and the wagons drove around the cabin so the first wagon on would be the first off. There were thirteen wagons on the boat when we crossed. We were the secon wagon on. The one in front of us was loaded with corn and our oxen eat corn all the way across.

We camped when we got across and some drunk men came by shooting thire guns. I was so scared. I fell flat on my stomach in the snow and lay there until Mother made me get up. We camped one night in the Wolf Swamp, the wolf howeld around our camp all night.

We crossed Black River twice. First at Poplar Bluff, Mo, than at Poachants [Pocahontas] Ark. We forded Current River at Doniphan, Mo. Poplar Bluff and Doniphan were very small towns then. Then we went to Walnut Ridge, Ark and seen our first cotton in the fields. We children thought it was so pretty, we had Dad stop the wagon so we could get some of the pods, that was what we called the cotton bolls.

The last night we camped in a little log cabbin, didn't have no floor but had a big stick and dirt chmbly [chimney] with a big fire place. The snow was about two feet deep.

Dad gave me a dime that night to wash his feet. I felt ritch. I had 20 cents for I had found a dime one night where we had camped.

We left Ky in Sept 1890, arrived at Walnut Ridge, Ark Jan 1st 1891. We were all so well and healthy when we got to my uncles who had lived in them swamps. They were so sickly looking, I wouldn't let them tuch me. Mi mother scolded me. I said I wasn't going to let them kiss me.

We stayed there until the next fall. We all got sick having chills and Dad said he wouldn't live where his family was sick, so he loaded the wagon and we came to Riply, [Ripley] County at Poynor, MO where he traded his oxen for a team of horses and homesteaded 40 acres of land where he lived the rest of his life. I was the last child to leave home at the age of 19. I was marred, raised eight children and have twenty-five grandchildren and twenty-one great grandchildren."

Not long after Granny wrote this story for me, she had a massive stroke and was not able to speak or walk again.

SIXTEEN

EMMA JEAN

Lake City, Colorado, Spring 1978

There wasn't much to do on gray days when it snowed. Peter headed for the high country to take photographs, and I learned to make elk chili and fry pink trout we'd caught in hidden mountain lakes. One winter afternoon while Peter hunted for beaver around Lake San Cristobal, I visited one of our new friends, Emma Jean Vickers, Perk's wife. She and Perk lived across Highway 149 in a log cabin nestled beneath Red Mountain, another fourteen-thousand-foot peak. He built the first room to their cabin, and they had lived there since they married in 1945.

Emma Jean wasn't native to this part of the country. After she and Perk said "I do," she left the comforts of her Texan family to join her gold-miner husband in Lake City, entering a primitive life without electricity, television, telephones, paved roads, indoor plumbing, running water, doctors, or nurses. Her new life was a rude awakening for the young, well-mannered bride trained in classical music. There was nothing in the mountains for her except her love for a man, clean air, and beautiful scenery.

"When we married, all we had was this one room," Emma Jean said as she waved her hand around like a symphony director, showing me the cabin. "We didn't have a very good roof either, and one day, in came a big rain." She pointed up, and her clear blue eyes flickered as she sorted through years of memories.

I looked around the cabin and noticed the enormous hand-chiseled logs that stretched across the ceiling the entire length of the living room. The head of a monster bull elk with a twelve-point rack hung above the fireplace. Perk shot it back in '29. Shafts of light filtered through the picture window on the front of the cabin and cast a golden tone on the spruce walls, green plants, and mementos. Through the window, I could see my and Peter's little cabin on a hill on the other side of the Lake Fork of the Gunnison River.

"I only had three pots and pans," Emma Jean went on, "and I had them sittin' around catching the pourin' rain, and . . . umm, Ol' Norman came over to see me."

She explained that Norman was a visitor from Oklahoma, and in those days, people dropped in often and without notice. The man saw the rain dripping down from the ceiling and told Emma Jean not to worry, he could fix the leak in a quick minute.

"Then Ol' Norman pulled out his .44 and aimed it down at the floor and shot right in front of me!" she exclaimed. "He shot a hole about the size of a toothpick and told me not to worry because the rain would go right through there."

She chuckled in short, throaty laughs and took a deep draw on her cigarette. "Of course, it just drained and drained," she smiled.

Emma Jean wanted to know if I played bridge, but I hadn't played cards since college and had forgotten most of the game. I didn't want to embarrass myself, or her, but she insisted because there was nothing else to do during long winters in the San Juans, where everyone became a prisoner to the weather.

"Any time we can get four people who can hold thirteen cards together then we got a game," she said. "And sometimes it doesn't even matter if you talk."

Emma Jean was unusually shy but quick-witted and full of funny one-liners. She often stared out the window as dust particles hung in streams of light, and we sat in silence as we played. There was something tender and insecure about her; she seemed far away, absorbed in her own world. She rarely spoke at all, and I wondered if that was because she was an introvert or if isolation in the San Juans had demanded a vow of silence. After a few weeks of being snowbound in Lake City, I understood what it meant to be quiet, even paranoid, being alone on top of the world. Whatever the case, Emma Jean was tight-lipped, which may have been for the best. I soon learned the importance of keeping your mouth shut in Lake City. It was a small town, and everyone knew everyone else's business. Whatever anyone said or did became the news. The only other news was the weather.

One cold snowy day when I was in the empty ranch office to use the telephone, I heard someone playing a piano. I hung up the phone and peeked around the corner to see Emma Jean at an old upright piano behind a horse saddle. A deer head hung on the wall, and a water canteen dangled from one of the antlers. Emma Jean's hands floated skillfully across the keyboard as sweet notes from the piano drifted and evaporated in the thin air. I could tell she was a maestro as I stood and listened quietly. Her face shone as she looked out the window toward the Continental Divide. The music moved like a healing balm through me:

"When I look down from lofty mountain grandeur, and hear the brook and feel the gentle breeze, then sings my soul, my Savior God to Thee . . . How great Thou art!"

She must have sensed someone was in the room because she stopped abruptly and turned around. When she saw me standing there, she blushed and quickly retreated into her diffidence. I felt awkward, like I had intruded on her private space or discovered her secret identity. It was such a privilege; no one on earth had ever heard of this timid mountain woman, a classically trained musician hidden from the world. I was in the presence of genius. Emma Jean scurried away from the piano and rushed out of the office. I tried to compliment her on her way out, but she brushed me aside.

"Ah, anything in the key of C, I've got it," she said smiling, before disappearing out the door and into the cold.

I thought about Emma Jean the rest of the day and night, how she had carved meaning and purpose, made art, out of such a rudimentary existence. I wondered what dreams she'd left behind. Had she done all the things she'd wanted? Was she happy? Didn't she want the world to hear her play? By outward appearances, Emma Jean had everything. She had a long, fruitful marriage, grown children, grandchildren, a valuable ranch in the Rockies, anything money could buy. She was well-known and respected in her tiny community. Obviously, she had accepted her lot in life, which made me wonder about my own. If she was able to find happiness and make peace secretly playing for the mountains, why couldn't I?

In past generations women didn't "find themselves." The path to success and security was marriage and family. But I was full of dreams and ambitions. I wanted to be more than a silly goose, a country girl, a man's appendage, a vessel for babies. I tried to be submissive and follow my husband's commands, but it wasn't working. Not for either of us. I read how women in the Bible were encouraged to have calm and gentle spirits because such was true beauty to God. Of course I wanted to be beautiful, but the calmer and gentler I became, the angrier Peter got. There was something alive in me that he could see, even when it stayed dormant. Whatever I was doing or not doing didn't bring happiness to either of us, and I was baffled. I really was trying to be the perfect pious wife. I decided to carry on and continued hoping things would work out, but a smoldering fire burned inside me. God knew the truth, that I wanted to kick Peter's Yankee ass.

SEVENTEEN

A TICKET TO RIDE

Poplar Bluff, Missouri, 1965

The Poplar Bluff High School mascot was a happy-looking mule, and Missourians loved and honored the animals because of their strength and their hardy, obstinate nature. Mother always said I was as stubborn as a mule, and she was right. They weren't elegant animals, but they were tough and dependable and pulled the plows that tilled the land that fed us. They were necessary and not to be taken for granted.

In 1965, the Beatles were the hottest group in America, and their song "A Ticket to Ride" was the number-one hit on the radio. The lyrics often stuck in my head: "She's got a ticket to ride, and she don't care"—and neither did I at seventeen. I wanted a new, different, and exciting life. I was determined to get away from South Eleventh Street, from my rollaway bed, from Mother's constant disapproval, and from feeling like an ugly duckling.

"My God, you're a dunce!" she'd say.

Mother's words were a jagged knife in my already fractured self-image. My body was gangly and needed to take shape. My hips were too wide, my breasts too small, my hair too curly, my eyes blind and small, my lips narrow and tight, my feet too big. I was clumsy and self-conscious and wore thick, black-rimmed glasses because I was nearsighted and legally blind. My hormones exploded in awkward and out-of-control ways. I remember a boy once called me "gorilla" because my arms and legs were covered in thick, black hair that made me look like an ape. I begged Mother for permission to shave my legs, when I turned thirteen, otherwise, it would take a bush hog to mow them.

"Once you start that business, there ain't no stoppin'," Mother cautioned. "You'll have to keep at it."

Her answer sounded like permission to me, maybe even compassion. I ran to the bathroom and shaved my legs as fast as I could and then discovered that underneath all that hair I had legs whiter than bleached sheets. Instead of a hairy gorilla, I looked like a slick, shiny, albino monkey.

I also had a problem with the hair on my head. It was thick and kinky curly. Since we couldn't afford a trip to the hair salon, Mother kept my hair short in a boy-cut. She said it was easier to comb and manage, but I dreamed of long, flowing curls to make me look like a princess. Instead, Mother said I looked like a cow.

I believed I was going to die unless something changed in my life. My self-image was wounded, and my spirit was fading. No one had any idea how much I wanted to escape. As a sweet, compliant, churchgoing girl who didn't drink, smoke, have sex, or hang out with wild kids, I was ready to break every restraint and blast off to the moon.

When I was old enough, I stayed away from home as much as possible. Between school, babysitting, and drama club, I kept occupied and busy. I even got an after-school job at the public library for fifty cents an hour. In an attempt to make Mother happy, I saved enough to buy a set of dishes at Montgomery Ward. I put them on layaway and made payments each week until I paid off the forty dollars. Mother had never owned matching dishes, and though she never said so, I guess she liked the new ones. They stayed in the cupboard. When I was a kid, we never used nice things except for special occasions.

I also went to church. Three times a week I attended South Poplar Bluff General Baptist, not because I was a religious nut but because church was a safe place to escape. I had been attending church since Mother allowed me to go to an old-time revival. It had been a hot summer night, and I'd hoped the revival had games and refreshments for kids my age. I was eleven at the time.

The Little Black River Baptist Church was a one-room building in the country with wooden floors, straight-backed pews, a piano, and a podium. The ledger showed thirty-three people attended the previous Sunday. Old hillbilly farmers and their wives sang from worn-out hymnals. Men crooned and women warbled. Kids squirmed. Everyone sang, "Take my hand, Precious Lord, Lead me home."

The evangelist began preaching and flailed his arms, shouted, and sweated like a farmer behind a plow. He read Scriptures about heaven and hell. He shouted they were both real. I learned some people attended revivals because things happened. It was more exciting than the movies. Sometimes people hollered and danced in the aisles. The preacher, rotund and dressed in a suit and tie, stomped his feet and slammed the Bible on the podium. When he did, I jumped. He sprayed spit in the air and wiped his mouth with a handkerchief, pacing back and forth, preaching for another hour until he suddenly stopped and stood in front of the people. Quietly. Reverently.

"Ain't nobody guaranteed tomorrow. You ain't, and I ain't! Yer life can change in an instant. You could get killed in a car wreck on the way home. So if you died tonight, where would you spend eternity?"

He laid the Bible on the podium and looked longingly across the room. His eyes were on me, I just knew it.

He watched for movement among the people. "You ain't done nothin' too bad for the Lord to forgive. Lay down your burdens. It's time to repent and be saved!"

A hush came over the congregation as the pianist hit a few dead keys on the piano. Everyone sang, "Just as I am, without one plea, that Thy blood was shed for me, and that Thou bid'st me come to Thee, Oh, Lamb of God, I come. I come."

"I'll meet you here at the altar," the preacher said. "I won't embarrass you because you are the apple of God's eye."

My heart beat so fast I worried it would jump out of my chest. I was too young to think about the hereafter, yet I wrestled with my thoughts. I told myself I hadn't robbed a bank or killed anyone, didn't smoke or steal things. I was a good girl who obeyed my parents, most of the time, so why did I feel so nervous?

A gentle current escorted me down the aisle toward the altar, where humble folks were on their knees praying. When I finally reached the altar, everything moved in slow motion. An old woman in a cotton print dress with gray hair in a bun smiled and took my hand. She reminded me of Granny, and when she wrapped her arms around me, I fell into them. Suddenly, a wave of total approval embraced me, and I started to bawl like a calf as I buried my face in the biggest bosoms I'd ever seen.

The preacher spoke softly about Jesus dying for our sins. Would Jesus really die for a scatterbrained, dim-witted Essie Drowns like me? I didn't know, but I didn't have anything to lose. So I told God I was sorry for everything I could think of and then some. I was sorry for fighting with Jimmy, being jealous of Vicky, and resenting my mother. To my surprise, I felt lighter. A burden I didn't understand was gone. In that moment everything glowed, and I felt fresh, clean, and safe. This must have been what the preacher meant by being saved.

When I returned home from the revival, I tiptoed into our house on South Eleventh Street. The sounds of crickets and tree frogs filled the night air, and fans hummed in the windows while everyone slept. A train whistled in the distance. I heard Daddy snore as I slipped into my rollaway bed. Vicky was fast asleep. I felt better than when I took a bath with Ivory soap. I was eager for morning so I could tell Granny everything that had happened. She would understand.

I thought about what the preacher had said—that all the angels in heaven rejoiced when one little lamb was found. Maybe they were rejoicing over me. I didn't know, but a spiritual and moral compass came into my life that night. Just as I drifted off to sleep, I heard a lonesome train whistle in the distance and wondered what Mother would think of me now.

Going to church was how I discovered I was an extrovert. I came alive around others. I enjoyed talking, giggling, asking endless questions, and making jokes, but I couldn't be like that at home. Church was more than a mile on foot from my house, but it was without a doubt worth the walk. Rain or shine, I never missed a service or activity after that night.

Not long after I turned sixteen, Daddy surprised me with a used car. I have no idea how he paid for it unless he bartered mechanical work or it was payment from a truck driver. It was a 1950s Morris Minor, a little British two-door car about the size of a VW Beetle that looked like a miniature gangster car. It was the first thing in my life that made me feel cool. Once I had wheels, I had freedom, and I practically lived at South Poplar Bluff General Baptist.

Since I attended church by myself, I stood out. The pastor, Reverend Curtis Eaker, and his wife, Laverne, took me under their wings. I wasn't much older than their kids, but the pastor's wife noticed I was exceptionally mature and responsible for my age. She didn't know it was an act. I pretended to be mature and acted forty instead of sixteen. I needed acceptance so badly that I was overly compliant. I figured that if I were perfect no one would notice I was dim-witted or smack me with a leather belt. For the first time in my life, I was respected, even admired.

I assumed every preacher's wife played the piano, taught Sunday school, read the Bible an hour per day. I was sure Laverne Eaker would think I was going to hell if she heard me swear like the hillbilly boys on South Eleventh Street or knew how badly I wanted to smack them and Mother upside the head. But I was wrong. Laverne was a total surprise. She was boisterous, outgoing, and spontaneous, and her laughter was contagious. She was more fun to be around than any of the girls my age.

A few times we sang in a trio at church. Laverne was a good alto, but I screeched like a wounded cat and had to lip-sync most of the lyrics. Although I heard good pitch, I couldn't carry a tune. She didn't yell or make me feel stupid about it. Instead, she invited me to the parsonage for lunch on Sundays after church because families ate at home in the 1960s. Restaurants weren't on every corner in Poplar Bluff, and no one could afford to eat out anyway. Laverne would pop a beef roast or chicken with vegetables in the oven on Saturday so the meal was ready when church was over the next day. She made the most delicious banana and chocolate cream pies, but I never mentioned them to Mother, who also made wonderful pies. Laverne became my friend, a loving mother figure. Church became a place of emancipation. I hoped it was just a taste of the freedom to come.

One day in summer, I stood with a small group on the banks of Black River in east Poplar Bluff and sang hymns in the sunshine as we waited to be baptized. We held hands at the river's edge and walked down the boat ramp and slipped into the water. When it was my turn to go under, the pastor placed a handkerchief over my mouth and dipped me in the cold river in the name of the Father, the Son, and the Holy Ghost. When I came out of the water, my plaid dress ballooned around me like an inflated raft, ready to carry me downstream. I sputtered and wiped my eyes and was ready to float away. I was excited about whatever lay around every bend ahead. All things were new.

EIGHTEEN

NEAR DEATH ON ENGINEER PASS

The Rockies, Colorado, June 1978

The winter days were short, and it got dark around 3:30 p.m. Most afternoons, a blizzard came or at least a heavy snow, but when it didn't, we drove the two-lane highway to Gunnison and back to buy groceries—114 miles round trip. The journey was breathtaking. We curved through canyons and near rivers and snowy fields and spotted bighorn sheep, wolves, coyotes, and elk. One day, we saw so many bald eagles we lost count. We were mindful to head back to Lake City before dark because there was no way to call for help and the roads were deadly at night, but the drive to and from was exhilarating. I savored grocery shopping like it was high tea and loved the feeling of having lots of food and other comforts. Soon, the days of our pilgrimages to Gunnison, good neighbors, and glowing hearts would be behind us.

By March, Peter and I had settled into a daily routine of eating, sleeping, exploring aspen groves and secret lakes in the high country, and writing. Winter days turned into weeks and weeks into months as the manuscript for *A Walk Across America* grew slowly and laboriously to three hundred pages. Before we realized it, the days had become longer and the skies bluer. Wildflowers peeked through holes in the snow, and newborn calves played on the upper ranch at eleven thousand feet. It reminded me of *The Sound of Music*. Spring had arrived after its own long journey.

Perk's grandchildren played Superman and jumped off haystacks in their bare feet. Everyone was ready for warmer weather and new life. Peter and I would soon strap on our backpacks and leave our little log cabin that held so many sweet and sour memories. We had to wait for snow to melt in the higher elevations before we could leave Lake City. There were colossal glaciers and snow-packed fields above the timberline where we had to cross.

It wasn't until June 23, 1978, that we set off—perfect bikini weather in Florida but far different in the San Juan Mountains.

We stood in the sun and adjusted our backpacks as we prepared to meet over a hundred people at Lake City Park. Friends and neighbors were excited to walk nine miles with us, up a winding road through Henson Creek Canyon to Capitol City. We would follow the Alpine Loop, which was a backcountry route only accessible in the summer. We joked with Gary and Jean Wysocki and Phil and Carolyn Virden that we were almost finished walking across America and they were welcome to walk with us across Utah, Idaho, and Oregon. They laughed and passed on the invitation.

Getting back on the road was special. I hadn't felt that kind of group fellowship since my seminary days. So many friends chose to camp with us our first night back on the road that it felt like a family vacation. The idea of leaving made me heartsick. Everyone pitched tents in an open meadow at 9,480 feet on the site of Capitol City, a ghost town that flourished during the gold rush era in 1877. Back then, it had one of the most popular hotels in the whole mountain range. We managed to find the hotel, along with the remains of the post office building and a few brick kilns. We marveled over the fact that everything else in the boom town was gone.

The next day, more friends joined us, but it would be their final leg. The next few days of travel would prove treacherous for Peter and me. We savored the last moments with friends, hiking five miles higher to 11,200 feet, then stopped at another ghost town called Rose's Cabin, where friends from Lake City would arrive for a final send-off picnic.

In the heyday of Rose's Cabin, travelers came by stagecoach and stayed in one of the twenty-three rooms at the hotel, drinking themselves silly at night, playing poker, and eating from a table supplied with the best. It was fitting that we shared our last meal in a famed and bygone town with the best food and people in Lake City.

Perk and Emma Jean arrived with steaks for everyone, while others brought covered dishes of baked beans, salad, vegetables, garlic bread, sodas, and champagne. A reporter from Channel 9 News in Denver joined the group to film our goodbye toast to the Vickers, the Brocks, the Virdens, the Wysockis, Tom Ortenburger, Liz Warren, Tom Gross, Jed Vickers, Tom Baer, Jay Dickman, and many more. After we ate and shared lots of laughs, we lifted our glasses of bubbly for a farewell toast that made me more light-headed than the high altitude. Everyone felt like family, and I didn't know it at the time, but we would never see some of them again due to distance, changing circumstances, and death. I took a deep breath to hold back tears as we embraced, shook hands, and said our farewells. Peter and I waved to our friends, turned, and headed toward the glaciers that towered above us.

The climb got difficult quickly. We walked slowly away from the green meadows, rushing streams, and pine forests toward a harsh alpine environment, climbing higher and higher with each step. Ahead of us lay the most rugged terrain we had ever crossed, and where dangerous twists and turns meant we had to be sure-footed. Even trees didn't dare grow that high up. It was too dry and cold. The ground was too frozen. All that existed to welcome us above the timberline was a blanket of dwarf shrubs, marshes, grasses, mosses, and lichen.

We huffed and puffed, struggling in the oxygen-deprived air, trying to rest on twenty-foot-tall snowbanks and search for a place to cross the dangerous snow-packed Engineer's Pass, a notoriously treacherous but essential stretch. Following the position of the sun, we relied on our intuition and prayed we were going in the right direction, because any roads and trails were buried. The original road that connected Lake City to Ouray, our next destination, was built in 1877, and for one hundred years, travelers were warned to use extreme caution because of the frequent and unexpected avalanches, heavy snowfalls, and landslides. It was hazardous country, and there was no way to prepare for it.

At dusk, we still hadn't reached our goal, the peak of Engineer Pass, but we were bone-tired and decided to continue our search for the summit the next morning. Our lungs worked hard to breathe at twelve thousand feet, and adrenaline pumped in our bodies as we struggled to set up the tent in high winds on frozen ground. We found a flat spot and stacked rocks on top of the stakes to secure our tent. Thankfully, our Jansport sleeping bags were rated at minus twenty degrees, so we stayed toasty-warm zipped inside as we lay exhausted and quickly fell asleep.

Sometime during the night, we were awakened by hurricane-force winds and biting cold air against our faces, which were no longer covered by our sleeping bags. Although it was June, howling gusts beat against our nylon tent and pushed the dome roof all the way down to our bodies. Blowing snow, sleet, and hail pelted us all night long. We wrapped ourselves tighter and tighter, praying to keep dry so we didn't end up a pair of iced mummies. I remembered the lightning storm that hot night in The Breaks in Texas, and this was equally dangerous, but killer cold. I was afraid to go to sleep but nodded off between howls of wind and rushes of sleet and rain. The sun woke us the next morning, cheerful and bright, mocking the perilous night we'd endured. We broke camp wordlessly with our stiff, cold bodies and set out to find a route over the pass, trudging higher for another two hours, sunk into snow up to our knees.

At long last, we stood like tired, victorious warriors on top of Engineer Pass, one of the highest and most rugged passes in Colorado. Peter and I looked at each other, and it felt like we had conquered our own Mount Everest. I pulled off my reflector sunglasses and took it all in, eyes stinging in the wind. At thirteen thousand feet, we saw brilliant blue skies, a fluorescent sun, powerful gusts, and a vast wilderness of ice-mantled peaks that circled us. It was breathtaking.

———————

"We should get going," Peter said.

He was right. It was too cold and too dangerous to linger, so we searched for a way to trek down the other side toward Ouray.

Snow drifts were deep and dangerous as we walked on horizontal ice shelves, testing each step to make sure the ground would hold us. We inched along slowly, risking our lives with each step. Just as I started to feel nimble and cat-like, I lost my footing. Like a bobsled with no time to react at the starting line, I slid at breakneck speed for twenty feet straight down the side of the glacier, stopping inches from the edge of a steep cliff. I looked up, stunned that I had not fallen to my death. My backpack was caught on a jagged, hook-shaped piece of ice. Jansport had snatched me from the precipice. I laid on my back for a few minutes to catch my breath and gather my wits.

I slowly and carefully rolled over on my stomach and tried to find Peter. He was high above me, looking like a ghost. There was no way for him to get to me, so he coached and assured me as calmly as he could.

"Take it easy," he quavered.

He tried to act brave and hide his concern, but I could tell he was as scared as I was. I clawed into cracks in the ice with my stiff, frozen fingers and prayed my movement did not start an avalanche. I wished my hiking boots had cleats to grip the ice.

Finally, I grasped Peter's extended hand. He pulled me next to him and we embraced, knowing we'd almost lost each other. Again. I could feel his heart through his thick, goose down–filled parka. It was too dangerous, cold, and windy to linger on the narrow ice ledge. Like always, we took a deep breath, and without saying a word, we picked up our packs and kept walking. One thing was certain: I didn't want to live without the man who pulled me up from the rim of a deadly mountain cliff, regardless of our quarrels. There had to be a reason we kept coming back from the edge.

Ouray was hidden somewhere below us; all we could do was hope we were headed in the right direction. Once again, we followed the sun and our instincts across snowfields and glaciers until we dropped in elevation and saw melted spots on a remote one-lane road. We were almost there. The entire distance from Lake City to Ouray was only thirty-five miles on the Alpine Loop, but faced with the peril of crossing mountains on foot, it felt like a year had passed. To date, those miles were the most dangerous and the most spectacular.

We camped early and the next day hiked effortlessly down into Ouray at 7,792 feet. The thick, sweet air at the lower elevation made us feel energetic and hungry as bears, ready for a hot meal. I felt renewed, filled with promise, and thankful for my relentless husband and a sturdy backpack.

NINETEEN

YELLOW ROSES

Poplar Bluff, Missouri, 1965

During high school, I was boy crazy, but no one knew it because I was shy and too embarrassed to flirt. Cute cheerleaders and popular majorettes giggled, batted their eyelids, and wore miniskirts, while football players and muscular hunks swarmed them. Hunks steered clear of me. My arm pits were geysers of sweat that soiled my dresses. Because I perspired like a man, I wore underarm sweat guards to keep from staining my clothes and looking like a field hand. The clothes I wore were homemade or from flea markets, which added to my embarrassment.

All through my teenage years, my mind screamed, "You're a big cow! You're stupid! You aren't cute, witty, or smart enough to carry on a conversation with a boy."

I prayed that someday a man would fall in love with me and think I was beautiful, but I doubted that he lived anywhere near South Eleventh Street.

The summer I was sixteen, a florist delivered a dozen yellow roses to my house, and they were for me. I was flabbergasted.

Twelve roses? All for me?

I was so surprised that I ran across the backyard to Granny's shack and screamed at the top of my lungs. I held the bouquet as high in the air as I could, like I had won a trophy in an Olympic game.

"Look! Look, what I got!" I screamed with excitement.

I didn't care that the boy who sent them was from church and not one of the popular boys I dreamed about from school. Suddenly, I wondered if he liked me more than as a friend. Mother commented that a dozen roses cost a lot of money and told me to put them in water before they wilted.

"Oh! I want to keep them forever and ever," I said. I was giddy and flippant.

"Humph! I know you better than you know yourself," Mother said. Her eyes looked straight through me like an X-ray machine, and I was convinced she read my every thought.

"You're fickle!" she said. "And flighty!"

Did she just call me names? How could she know about all the boys I had crushes on? How could anyone? This was one of my best-kept secrets. I had crushes on Bobby, Clifford, Mike, Jim, Eddy, Homer, Amos, David, Hugh, Cletis, and more. I liked every cute boy who crossed my path or even looked at me. There were so many I don't remember their names. I had a fleeting thought, *What if I really am fickle? What if I turn out to be a slut?*

That scared me. How did Mother know I fell in and out of love with a look or a smile? They were mere fantasies, of course. I was too insecure, hairy, and sweaty to do anything other than imagine.

Mother appeared indifferent about the dozen roses. She wasn't much older than me when she started raising kids and was disappointed because Daddy worked seven days a week. I gushed over the flowers and didn't notice the look on her face or the pain in her heart. I don't believe anyone ever sent her a dozen roses, not even Daddy.

My school yearbook was called *The Bluff*. It was hotly anticipated, and when copies arrived, the entire graduating class raced around trading them for notes and signatures. As a member of the drama club, I was thrilled to receive the Best Actress Award. I was in several popular plays throughout school. Mother only attended one and claimed I went overboard and was too dramatic. She discouraged me from pursuing a career in theater.

"You'll end up just like Elizabeth Taylor with half a dozen husbands," she huffed, looking at my copy of *The Bluff*. "Just look what acting did for her!"

Mother didn't understand that drama gave me an alter ego, an escape from her criticism, from feeling unwanted. I'd just played the tight-lipped and grim old maid Judith Bickle in *A Man Called Peter*, an adaptation of a bestselling book, and had done an admirable job. I watched her scan the comments the boys in drama club had written.

"I must say that your 'Judith' was the best bit of characterization and acting this year. I truly consider you the perfect lady . . . You are the only one who has not shattered my 'perfect lady' image."

"I really admire you very much for many reasons."

"I have never met such a lovely creature with such a unique character and disposition in all of my born days. Always stay as sweet as you are now, and the world will always be at your feet."

Mother didn't seem interested in anything I did, and she really didn't like when anyone paid me a compliment, but I tried to ignore her detachment.

Acting covered the iron will that grew inside me and the desire to run from everyone's perception. I wasn't the lovely, proper creature they thought I was, and I didn't want to be. I was just pretending, behaving myself long enough to get by. I wanted to be wild, like the girls with long, blond hair and lots of cleavage. I wanted to be cute and fun and sexy. Still, I looked in the mirror and saw thick cat-eye glasses, a pointed nose, tight curls, and dim-witted Essie Drowns. I was displeased with how God had made me. I was surely in an imperfect body, in a defective family, on the wrong side of the tracks. But I was going to find the right place. When I stared out the window, the Beatles sang me an anthem, as they had many times before: "She's got a ticket to ride, and she don't care."

After I graduated from high school, I was going to leave South Eleventh Street, my rollaway bed in the lean-to bedroom, and Mother's harsh words, and I wouldn't look back except to blow kisses at Granny and Grandad.

TWENTY

HIGHER UP

The Great Basin Desert, July 1978

The contrast in geography and climate nearly killed us. We had dropped out of the tundra and glaciers into a desert valley on the western side of the Rockies, and it was hellish hot. We'd gone from green pine forests and happy valleys to arid, barren deserts. The change seemed to happen at lightning speed, even on foot. It was 118 degrees in Delta as we walked northwest in a heat haze, the bottoms of our feet burning through the soles of our hiking boots.

Colorado wasn't supposed to be like this, I thought, but the western part of the state was a high desert. My arms and legs were singed, my lips were dry and cracked, and my eyelids were so scorched it became difficult to blink. The canteens of water that used to last all day at the higher elevations were like teacups here. How quickly we had forgotten Texas and New Mexico. We weren't prepared with enough fluids to make it to the next town, and I was unable to ration what we did have. In the Great Basin

Desert, I drank water too quickly and was completely dehydrated and sapped of strength for the rest of the journey.

Somewhere along the road, I experienced a mirage. A rushing, sparkling stream of water appeared before me like a piece of heaven, and I was crazy enough with thirst that I stumbled over and fell to the ground to drink out of it. It was actually an irrigation ditch. Peter yelled at me not to drink the water, but I was going to faint from heat exhaustion, and I couldn't help myself. I guzzled water from the gully laced with cattle urine, parasites, and pesticides and started vomiting before I even made it back to the road. Mirages were a sly trick of the desert to keep human predators at bay. And they were effective. I should have known better.

Luckily, a state trooper drove by and saw me heaving on the side of the road. I was still faint and half-mad but knew the officer was for real. He knew who we were and stopped to help. We were the topic of conversation at every truck stop and on every CB radio in the area, and he'd probably seen us on TV and in the newspaper as well. And in God's name, who else would be out there?

I was too sick to walk when Trooper Tom Wuff took us in his patrol car to the nearest cheap motel where I vomited all night. Peter was sympathetic but reminded me that he had told me not to drink out of the ditch. Thankfully, he didn't complain about having to hole up in a motel.

By the next morning, I was weak and several pounds lighter but managed to walk eight miles to Grand Junction, near the Utah border. I had good reason to keep going. It was July 8, 1978, Peter's twenty-seventh birthday. Today of all days, beneath the layers of dirt and sweat, I wanted him to see the woman he fell in love with. I still couldn't hold a tune, but I sang "Happy Birthday" to him

and gave him a wristwatch I'd hidden in my backpack, a gift I'd
purchased secretly in Lake City. He preferred to keep time by the
location of the sun but claimed he liked it anyway. He was trying
and I was, too, although we were tired and irritated. Thankfully, the
exhaustion didn't allow us the energy to snap at each other.

We weren't even out of Colorado, and although I'd already suffered
a near-heatstroke and that hallucination, much worse was yet to
come. The deserts of Utah were notoriously punishing. Ahead of
us loomed arid badlands and rattlesnakes, naked country with no
places to seek shelter. We would need help if we were going to
survive the hundred-mile stretches between gas, food, and water,
so we hatched a plan to get some.

Outside Grand Junction, we found a rest-stop telephone
booth and scanned the Yellow Pages for someone we thought
might be able to support us through the hell of our next chapter.
Randomly, Peter called the First Assembly of God Church to ask
if a congregant would be willing to bring us water until we reached
Green River, Utah. We were on the front page of the local *Daily
Sentinel* that day, so thankfully the pastor of the church knew our
telephone call was for real. He instantly invited us to speak at his
service that night, so we cleaned up as best we could in a motel
room and walked to the church to speak to the congregation. We
shared a few stories and our plans to end the walk across America
somewhere off the coast of Oregon. The people were rapt, and by
the end of the night, we had several volunteers.

The next day, we walked along Old Highway 50 and crossed the
border into Utah, which was named after the Ute nation and meant

131

"those that are higher up." We certainly didn't feel "higher up." There was nothing but empty desert in every direction—boiling sun, baked rock, sand, and flats. Whirlwinds of dust danced across the landscape. The sun cooked the pavement to 132 degrees. I was grateful we had full canteens and help checking in on us. I didn't know if we would survive, as the gnats and flies surrounded us. They swarmed me. I didn't have the energy to lift my arms to swat them away, so I picked up a small tumbleweed and stuck it under my hat to cover my face. I pretended it was a fancy hat with a net, and whenever the gnats tried to reach my face to suck up what little moisture I had, I turned my head back and forth to knock them away.

It was almost 4:00 p.m. when the good Samaritans from the church in Grand Junction pulled up in a truck. We had not eaten all day, and Peter was as drained as I was. Ron Maupin and Jim Easterly brought us six big hamburgers, French fries, soft drinks, cake, and a cooler full of water. Perishable food was as good as gold. We sat under a bridge and ate like starved dogs. They told us twenty-two people had died that day in Texas due to the heat wave. It was 114 degrees there, and I couldn't understand how we were alive in Utah, where temperatures were even higher.

"Good luck," they told us.

I could tell they were conflicted about leaving. We'd be camping for days before we hit the next town.

It was no surprise that 66 percent of Utah was government land, I thought as we dragged our scorched bodies along Interstate 70 toward Green River. This desert was good for nuclear test sites and aliens, and in my opinion that was all. There were no side roads to walk along, so travelers honked and waved as they zoomed past us on the interstate in their air-conditioned cars and big rigs. No doubt we gave the truckers plenty to talk about. We must have looked crazier than hell with giant umbrellas attached to our backpacks for shade, not to mention I had a bush over my face. I didn't care what anyone thought because the scorching sun and crust-covered earth sucked the life and water out of my body, and yes, we were crazier than a cross-eyed squirrel to be out there.

By the time we made it into town, Peter and I were annoyed with each other. We'd walked twenty-three miles the day before and only had one cup of water and an apple between us. Green River was a solitary crossroads, once the stomping ground for Butch Cassidy and his wild bunch. Now it was a watering hole for people who visited the Arches and Canyonlands National Parks.

The best thing about Green River was that Peter's parents and little sisters, Betsi and Abby, were meeting us for their family vacation. We planned to hold up for a week in a motel to rest, eat, and spend time with his family. Peter's mom had never been west of the Mississippi River, and this sun-dried settlement would be an overwhelming culture shock, an entirely different, dusty planet from Greenwich, Connecticut, with its lush gardens and stately homes.

Peter hadn't seen his parents since the day we married in New Orleans, February 7, 1976, almost two years earlier. He missed them terribly. I hardly knew them at all. We met up in the lobby of our small motel, and Peter's mother burst into tears. Not because she was particularly proud of or happy to see her son (though she was) but because Peter looked like a charred lobster. It would have been hard for any mother to see. The road and sun above had scorched both of us into crust.

Mary Jenkins was in her fifties with clear blue eyes, translucent skin, and blond hair tied back in a bun. She had the spirit of a dove. Her sense of joy and excitement were pure and childlike, qualities Peter had as well, and among the reasons I loved him. I had never met a woman with such an honest, wonder-loving personality, and I adored her from the first time I met her. Betsi and Abby, Peter's preteen sisters, were cute and giddy and ready to jump in the motel swimming pool. They had been cooped up in a car since Connecticut, and their giggles and squabbles made life seem normal. They were radiant flowers to me, drops of dew in the desert.

Fred Jenkins was very different from Peter's mom. Peter loved to talk politics and current events with his dad, who was a huge and handsome man. He stood six-foot-three and had a mighty laugh and strong opinions to match—about people, government, celebrities, food, cars, money, and everything else. Since I had grown up with Mother, Fred felt familiar. He was fiery—one minute purring like a kitten, the next growling like a lion. He was extremely proud of his oldest son and smiled from ear to ear when he talked about Peter writing for *National Geographic* and the publication of our book *A Walk Across America*. He was happy about Peter's fame and the financial opportunities that lay ahead. I had never seen a bond between father and son like theirs and wondered if Peter's dad might have fawned over him a bit too much. I wondered if his younger brothers, Freddy and Scott, who were equally bright, handsome, fun, and adventurous, would have agreed with me.

We never know all the reasons people act the way they do, but Fred Jenkins turned out to be hard to understand. He was unpredictable with Mary. I witnessed him berate and belittle her during our trip, and it made me feel sad and angry and want to protect her. Sweet Mary would cry, wipe her tears, and make excuses for her husband's behavior, explaining that Fred had lost his mother when he was a boy and his family also lost their wealth during the Great Depression. He grew up in the shadow of what should have been. It didn't take long for me to see where Peter had learned how to throw verbal darts.

Fred hadn't wanted Peter to marry me, so I was quiet and reserved around him. He knew I was a hillbilly. He wrote Peter a letter before we married and claimed I was mentally slow. Since I was a little older than Peter, Fred accused me of robbing the cradle and being a gold digger. He believed I would keep his son from achieving fame and fortune.

My Ozark roots and hillbilly twang grated on him. I was able to turn a one-syllable word into two or three and end it with a twang. "Well, my Lord" became "Way-ell, my-aa, Low-w-aard!" I talked slower than the Yankees from the North; gushed about cornbread, coffee, and Jesus; and avoided arguments because like all people in the South, I was taught to be polite. If you didn't agree, you parted ways with "Bless your heart" and agreed to pray for each other. I often prayed for Fred. He simply couldn't understand why Peter had married someone like me, thinking I had nothing to offer. But he was mistaken to believe my hillbilly brain didn't work any faster than my Southern drawl.

Our drive through Arches National Park, dinners at the town's small restaurant, and dips in the pool were loud and full of laughter because of the little girls. I wanted a warm and caring relationship with my father-in-law, so I made like my Daddy and kept my distance and thoughts to myself. Like Peter, Fred was more bark than bite and had a tender streak, and pride stood in the way of who he really wanted to be.

When the week was over, the girls said their goodbyes to us, and Mary wept yet again. Fred gave Peter a bear hug and long handshake and quickly kissed me on the cheek. I was sad to see them go, but watching how Peter's father had treated his mother was a startling look into the future. Could I live like Mary? Was I already living like that? I was weighed down by a week of hearty food and questions I wasn't ready to answer when we hit the road yet again.

TWENTY-ONE

A MORMON MORTUARY

Provo, Utah, August 1978

The majority of Utah's population lives tucked against the Wasatch Mountain Range that ran north and south through the state. It was believed that over 60 percent of Utahans were Mormon at the time. Each street we walked in 1978 was squeaky clean and full of blue-eyed couples with perfect white teeth, followed by a half dozen fair-haired children. Provo was home to Brigham Young University (BYU) and actor Robert Redford's Sundance Resort. Salt Lake City lay forty miles ahead.

We had the opportunity to eat lunch at the BYU cafeteria, which both Peter and I were excited about. Being around academics energized me, and I was craving a glass of cold iced tea—not too sweet, just the kind I had enjoyed my whole life. Oh, how I missed Southern tea! We arrived as soon as the cafeteria opened, and I immediately ordered a beverage.

"I'll have a sweet tea," I smiled.

The young college waitress blushed and said she was sorry, but tea was not on the menu. Then I asked for iced coffee, and she started to stammer. When I finally asked for a Coke, she turned beet-red, and I thought she might faint. Then I remembered that Mormons were forbidden from drinking anything with caffeine. No tea, coffee, Cokes, chocolate drinks, or anything. Peter laughed uncomfortably and was embarrassed. I felt badly and was a little ashamed of my ignorance. At that point, I was ready to ask for a shot of Jack Daniels, but I settled on a glass of water.

I was fascinated to be in the belly of Mormon country because I had studied comparative religions while at the seminary in New Orleans. When we walked by a manicured cemetery, I was struck by the absence of crosses on headstones and steeples. Instead of church buildings with crosses on top of the spires, Mormons met in buildings called *wards* with the angel Moroni on top. Joseph Smith, the founder of Mormonism, said the angel Moroni appeared to him in 1823 and translated buried golden plates into *The Book of Mormon*. The tall golden figure with the trumpet to his lips symbolized the spread of Smith's gospel. And in Provo, he was everywhere.

Smith claimed Mormonism was the restored religion and that *he* was the true prophet. He said *The Book of Mormon* was the most correct book on earth and that men could become angels and gods like Jesus Christ. Dead people were saved through a rite called baptism of the dead, and salvation was possible without repentance. Jesus earned His way to deity. There was no Trinity and no original sin. Jesus and Lucifer were brothers. It shocked me in seminary and shocked me even more in pleasant, harmonious Provo. Joseph Smith's doctrines conflicted with everything I had studied about Christianity. Then there were his doctrines of polygamy and celestial marriages, which I chose to think about and research at another time.

Pregnant women lined the sidewalks going to and from their cars. They seemed to be everywhere. I wondered if having lots of babies was a requirement, since Joseph Smith taught that spirits waited in the cosmos to inhabit human bodies. I was fascinated by the culture. It was like visiting a foreign country, and I had many questions, probably inappropriate ones. I wondered if any of the young women lived in plural marriages. If so, were they happy? What was it like sharing your husband with other women? Officially, polygamy was only practiced until Utah became a state, but in some sects it was still alive and well. Utahans seemed normal—lovely, even—but I struggled to reconcile their theology. I couldn't help it. It had not been long since I was a student in Christian seminary, and if anyone read Genesis to Revelation, the differences between Scripture and *The Book of Mormon* were glaring. The Joseph Smith–revised King James Bible eliminated the doctrine of the Trinity, claimed Jesus was born in Jerusalem and not Bethlehem, and said six-foot men dressed like Quakers lived on the moon.[1]

On August 25, 1978, the day after my thirty-first birthday, we walked through Provo and Springville, its suburb. I'd been looking

1. https://www.christianstudylibrary.org/article/latter-day-saints-summary-and-evaluation-mormonism

forward to this day for the past month, and it felt like a belated birthday gift.

Peter yelled, "There she is!"

His oldest sister had come to meet us in Sandy, Utah, to hike for a few days. The bright, freckle-faced, redheaded Winifred was my sister-in-law, but I would have chosen her as a friend any day of the week. Everyone called her Winky; she smiled and laughed all the time. As soon as she saw us, she lit up like a Christmas tree.

The three of us walked and talked along a busy four-lane road just twelve miles from Salt Lake City. Winky was so excited she started to walk quickly. Calmly, I explained that a gentler pace was important to conserve energy, and I encouraged her to slow down. After walking from New Orleans to Utah, I had learned not to be tempted by speed. Maintaining stamina was the difference between making it to the next town or drinking from an irrigation ditch.

By midmorning, sweat dripped down our foreheads, and predictably, Winky and I lagged behind Peter. We hadn't eaten a thing and were hoping to reach a café or diner before we melted completely. It was already hot and sticky. Winky talked about scrambled eggs while I dreamed of pancakes. We agreed that a glass of cold, fresh-squeezed orange juice would be essential. The heat was already unbearable when I looked around and noticed a row of full, leafy trees across the road and called to Peter up ahead. I pointed at the trees and suggested we walk in the shade where it was cooler, especially since this was Winky's first day on the road.

Peter stopped and thought.

He didn't like the idea because our backs would be to the traffic. From the first day Peter and I left New Orleans, he had insisted that we walk facing traffic. He was reluctant about my idea but agreed, probably because he was outnumbered. Peter marched under the shade trees ahead of us while Winky and I laughed and talked, oblivious to him and the rest of the world. It was heaven.

We strolled on the much cooler, grassy shoulder and noticed a long concrete building to our right that was back off the road. It looked very institutional, a government building, maybe. It was surrounded by a huge green lawn and a neat collection of hedges. When we reached the entrance, the sign said it was a Mormon mortuary. We shrugged and kept moving.

Winky and I continued slowly up an incline when suddenly, behind us and out of nowhere, we heard skidding tires and a deafening screech. Unconsciously, I reached for Winky. The impact was hellish. There was no time to turn around to see what the powerful force was. Winky was thrown straight up in the air like a volleyball, and when she came down, she shattered a windshield and bounced to a landing spot about fifteen feet away.

The back door of the car slammed into my lower back hard enough that my body sunk itself into the metal before flying through the air, rolling and spinning like a rag doll. I skidded across the grass and ended up in a heap near Winky. We were on the lawn of the mortuary just inches from an above-ground gas line.

People came running from all directions. I heard a boy cry and Peter scream, "Who did this? Who did this?"

Groups of people huddled over us and talked in hushed tones while a man from the mortuary ran out and placed a silk pillow under Winky's head. She was going into shock. Another person held an umbrella over me to shade me from the sun. I heard myself whimper like a dog, not understanding why. I faded in and out, groaned and tried to move. An older man said he was a chiropractor and told me to be still. He touched my lower back, spine, and legs, and I overheard him tell Peter that my hips and back might be broken. His voice shook.

Peter yelled at the stranger to shut up, to get away from me, and to keep his thoughts to himself because I was conscious and could hear. My face was buried in the dirt, but I heard bits and pieces of everything through the sirens and ringing in my ears. At this point, all I could do was moan. Shortly, some men approached Peter and told him they saw what had happened. They said a pickup truck cut off a kid in a '74 Chevy. The car was forced off the road and ran into us.

Peter raced between Winky and me. He was frantic and screamed for people to get away from us. He didn't know how badly we were hurt, and his voice quivered as he assured me everything was all right and he would stay with me. He planted a kiss on my dirt-smeared face, and I felt loved. A trio of men in white picked me up and put me on a stretcher, loading me into an ambulance with Winky. Within seconds we were on our way to the emergency room. A medic leaned over me and lifted my eyelids as we sped through traffic. He smelled like medicine, but the smell of grass and dirt was stronger.

The thought hit me that I might be paralyzed. My body was shaking and jerking uncontrollably, and I couldn't move my legs. A big knot was lodged in my throat, and I tried to hold it together, but tears rolled down my face. It had all happened so fast. One second Winky and I were giggling, and the next we were thrown through the air like rubber dolls. I wondered if this was the end. Maybe I was dying.

"You all right, Barb?" Winky asked.

Her voice was faint as she reached across the ambulance for my hand. I looked over. Her red hair was covered in blood, grass, and rocks. She wore a neck brace, and her eyes were filled with pain. But she was smiling.

"Barb, you all right?" she asked again.

"I don't know." I didn't want to talk. "I hope so."

"The first time I come out to walk with you and Pete, and look what a big welcome I get," she said.

"Oh-o-o, Winky, I'm so sorry," I sighed.

She started to chuckle, "Thank God for big buns!"

Everything was jumbled in my head, and I didn't understand. "For what?"

"Our big rear ends!" Winky laughed.

I tried to laugh too, but it hurt. We held each other's hands all the way to the hospital until medics pulled us out of the ambulance and pushed us into the emergency room. Winky was wheeled to one room, and I was taken to another. The ER doctor poked, pushed, and examined me but never said a word. I feared the worst as my body turned blue and then black. People worked on me in silence, and it was breathtaking agony as nurses took my vitals, X-rays of my pelvis and back, and tested for internal bleeding. *Where the hell was Peter? And Winky?*

Dreadful minutes passed before a nurse pulled back the curtain and Peter walked in with the doctor. He was pale (underneath the sunburn). I feared my hips were broken. I might need surgery or end up paralyzed in a wheelchair for the rest of my life. I was convinced that my walk across America was over.

The doctor's body language was stoic and businesslike. His face didn't reveal a single clue. Finally, he said, "The X-rays show no broken bones, and there is no internal bleeding."

As soon the announcement was made, he turned and walked out.

The nurse raised her eyebrows, and the corners of her mouth tilted into a half smile. She whispered, "It really is a miracle! I've seen lots of people come in here after being hit by a car. I've never seen anyone hit at fifty miles per hour who walked away from it."

She told Peter and me that the medic in the ambulance said that if Winky and I had turned around to see the car that crashed into us, our faces and chests would have been crushed. In addition, if the car had skidded into us ten feet sooner, it would have hit the above-ground gas line, and all of us would have been blown to smithereens. Again, my stuffed and heavy Jansport backpack was a divine shield that saved my life.

Peter exploded in thanksgiving, "Praise the Lord!"

The doctor gave Winky the same report of no broken bones or internal bleeding, but she had a pulled neck muscle and needed to wear a brace for a few days. My body trembled so hard I couldn't sit up or dress myself without help, and I felt sick to my stomach. The nurse explained that I was in shock and likely to have the shakes and nausea all day.

Winky and I struggled as we stood upright and braced ourselves against Peter, limping down the hall past the nurses' station. The nurse who helped me get dressed stood in the doorway with amazement on her face and waved goodbye. She shook her head in disbelief as she watched us hobble back out into the Utah sun. We were in the hospital less than four hours total.

After all these years, there's still a knot where the car slammed into my backside. Thank God for big buns.

TWENTY-TWO

THE BUTTERFLY

School of the Ozarks, 1967

W e're nothin' but poor country people," had been drilled into my head from an early age.

Since we were hillbillies, my only path out of poverty and the stigma of being a bumpkin was to get the education Mother and Daddy didn't have. I never thought of them as ignorant because they were industrious, hard-working, and resourceful. They were big readers and listened to the daily news. Their eighth-grade diplomas were equivalent to high school diplomas today, but white-collar opportunities and social rank remained nonexistent for the likes of them. Hard physical labor was what kept the wolf away from South Eleventh Street. I grew up learning how to plant a big garden, never to buy anything on credit, and to squeeze a nickel until the buffalo hollered. But I was ready to learn more.

My parents were too poor to send me to college except for one option: a work-for-tuition, Presbyterian-affiliated, liberal arts college in western Missouri near the Arkansas border, called

School of the Ozarks. The campus sat on a high bluff overlooking the White River, 225 miles west of home. Admissions were highly competitive, as thousands of poor hillbilly kids like me applied. My brother, Jimmy, was a sophomore there, and if one family member got in, siblings were given priority. I crossed my fingers.

The campus sprawled over one thousand picturesque acres west of Branson. Students worked in the canning factory; made fruitcakes and jellies; produced flour and corn meal in the mill; and worked in the cafeteria, library, clinic, maintenance, and agriculture departments. The jobs covered living expenses, including college tuition. Critics said the School of the Ozarks' work program was nothing but indentured servitude. The school countered the criticism by saying young people needed to learn a good work ethic as well as get a good education. Working didn't bother me. I wasn't afraid to put the sweat in and was glad for the opportunity to get a college education. The *Wall Street Journal* said it was one of the best tuition-free private colleges in the United States and ranked as "one of the most unusual" liberal arts colleges in the country.

I was accepted and assigned to work twenty hours a week in the library, probably because I had referenced my job at the Poplar Bluff Public Library on my application.

Miss Mary Anna Fain was my boss, a persnickety spinster who acted more like a drill sergeant (on steroids) than a librarian. She was a tall, robust woman with gray hair pulled back in a bun, which accentuated her giant nose, big lips, and oversized glasses. She wore a tailored suit with a neck scarf and pearls every day. Her eyes snapped and she snorted with disapproval when a student arrived one minute late to work, but I liked her. For some reason, she liked me too. She was fascinating and almost adorable in a gruff way.

She demanded punctuality, orderliness, dependability, service, and loyalty. I had grown up following orders, so I was well-equipped for the likes of Miss Fain.

Mostly, I worked at the front desk and helped people check out their books while watching Miss Fain and her elephant-sized legs hustle across the lobby floor in her favorite pair of old-fashioned, wide-heeled pumps. She tried to tiptoe, but it never worked. She roamed the aisles looking for students who were whispering or worse. It was a serious offense to talk in the library, and God forbid you get caught kissing your boyfriend behind a bookshelf. When Miss Fain shook her head no and made a loud *shu-u-ush* to be quiet, you knew you were in trouble. If she pointed her finger at you, it might as well have been a loaded gun.

It wasn't long before I noticed the handsome young men who studied in the library, but of course, they didn't notice me. I wanted to be wild, charming, free, and fun, but I was scared. Mother said that I was simple and clumsy. I desperately needed help with my appearance and self-confidence as well as any information on men and dating.

The change began with academics, which came easier to me than hair and makeup. During my second semester I entered a political essay contest sponsored by Judge Walter Green. I'd never heard of him before, but he must have been important in this area of the Ozarks. I loved to write but was scared because contestants had to be interviewed by a panel of community leaders. My whole life I had been told I was silly and a dunce, but I mustered up enough courage to submit a paper called "Advantages of Democracy over Communism or Socialism," and to my total amazement, I was one of two winners. I figured it was because I used footnotes.

The second winner and I were flown to Washington, DC, where we attended a lawn party at a manor, toured a wax museum, and enjoyed a cruise down the Potomac River. I was living a fairy tale. It was the first time I had ever been to an airport or flown in a plane, the first time I'd tasted steak or stayed in a hotel. Our cruise on the Potomac River was unchaperoned, and we met two cute sailor boys who were on a weekend leave from the Navy base. It was a hypnotic and flirtatious evening over sandwiches and beer. I never liked the taste of beer, but I was seventeen years old, and it was a brave new world, so I tried. I was floating downriver talking to a handsome navy boy whom I knew I would never see again, and I was far, far away from South Eleventh Street. We kissed good night, and I liked it. When I got back to school, I asked my roommate, Pat Decker, if she'd show me how to style my hair.

Pat was cute, bubbly, and popular, and with her expertise, I traded my kinky tight curls for a popular short bouffant. From there, she helped me discard my black-rimmed, cat-eye glasses for contact lenses. It just so happened that her brother-in-law was an optometrist who let me make payments over time. Contact lenses were more than this poor hillbilly girl could afford, but I was determined to have them. I earned extra money cleaning houses, scrubbing, sweeping, dusting, and mopping the homes of professors for five dollars a day. I was proud when I was able to settle my debt. I couldn't ask my parents for help, and I was sure Mother would disapprove. She wrote once a month with news of Granny and Grandad, what was growing in the garden, and the weather. She always tucked two or three dollars inside the letter. I knew that was all she had, and I wished I didn't need it.

Each semester I gained confidence. I made friends, joined popular clubs, and earned top grades. I even started smoking because I thought it added flair and sophistication. Plus, nothing tasted better than a Coke with potato chips followed by a cigarette. A haze of smoke thick enough to kill a Clydesdale saturated our dorm room. Pat and I played 45 vinyl records, smoking, puffing, and smoking some more. I'm sure the stench was unbearable, but we were cool.

Before long, there wasn't a trace of Essie Drowns. I was finally leaving her behind and starting to become more of the girl I wanted to be. Music blared from our room. We danced, drank, and sang loud enough that the dorm mother had to knock on the door, frequently telling us to turn it down.

TWENTY-THREE

MAGIC VALLEY

Idaho, September 1978

W e stayed in a motel for a week after the car accident while I recovered. Winky was well enough to travel after a few days, so her friends picked her up in an old VW bus, and they headed back East, waving goodbye with REO Speedwagon blaring on the radio. My bones and butt were sore, and I had a purple bruise the size of a beach ball across my rear end, but it was time to get back on the road. I walked slower than usual and faced the traffic. Never again did I walk with my back to traffic.

We inched forward heading northwest, crossing from Utah into southern Idaho, where the sky, air, and land felt open, lighter, and different somehow. We had walked 183 miles north of the angel Moroni and the Mormon mortuary.

The horizon was sprinkled with ranches; grain elevators; lush fruit orchards; and bountiful crops of sugar beets, beans, potatoes, and corn. We entered Magic Valley, which spanned the Snake River Plain into the Sawtooth Mountains. It was "magic" because the dams and irrigation canal systems built at the turn of the twentieth century turned the volcanic ash into some of the greenest and most productive farmland in the United States. Water meant life and prosperity. Now, it was a fruited plain and a modern garden of Eden.

When Peter and I crossed the border, it was hard to believe Idaho had only been a state for eighty-eight years. Many of the people who homesteaded the land at the turn of the century were still living. The Oregon Trail crossed here, and pioneers had stopped in the valley because of what they saw. In all directions lay deep canyons, rushing rivers, pheasant, goose, duck, deer, and other wildlife. Pioneers must have figured Oregon and Washington couldn't be any better than Idaho, so they stopped in the wide valley and turned settlements into fruitful towns like Burley, Kimberly, Twin Falls, Filer, Buhl, Jerome, Wendell, and Boise.

It was September 19, 1978, when a flock of Canada geese flew overhead on their way south. They honked to let us know winter would be coming in six weeks. The temperature was already chilly as we made camp in tiny Burley under a black sky with no end. Above us, a universe full of stars popped and twinkled and ignited my imagination. The end of our long walk was only a few months away, and our future was wide open, exciting, and as mysterious as the Idaho night sky.

Maybe it was because of my fall at Engineer Pass in the Colorado Rockies or that I was hit by a car outside Salt Lake City and escaped the angel of death twice, but Peter seemed more attached to me than ever. He told me he was ready to be a father and asked me to throw away my birth control pills. It took a while to process what he'd said. We were homeless bickering nomads and carried everything we owned on our backs. I still had a big black bruise and knot on my backside from being hit by a car, and the last thing on my mind was getting pregnant.

We had not discussed starting a family before and I didn't know if I was ready, though my biological clock told me my eggs were numbered. Many of my friends already had two or three children, and in my hillbilly family, I was considered old to have my first child. My mother and grandmothers had their first babies before they turned twenty, when they were barely grown. Mother and Daddy said they had given up on becoming grandparents.

In my mind, pregnancy was not an option while I walked across the country, but I reasoned that since we were nearing the end of our journey, maybe I would stop taking the pills. Idaho and Oregon lay ahead, and by this time, two states seemed like a stroll in the park, so I threw away the birth control pills. It was highly unlikely that I would get pregnant under duress anyway. Then again, my hillbilly grandmothers ended up with a house full of youngins', birthing over a dozen babies between them with the help of neighbor women who cured colic and childhood ailments with herbs and weeds, Ozark healing potions that would one day be passed down to my sister, Vicky.

———

Not long after we crossed into Idaho, a stranger who had read about us in the newspaper found us on the highway and introduced himself as Jack Ramsey. He was a respected banker and invited us to his lovely home in a tiny town west of Twin Falls called Filer. He and his wife, Lucy, lived on a quiet street lined with trees that glistened in fall colors, giant maple trees flickering red and orange against a powder-blue sky. Their neighborhood looked like a postcard from the small-town America of my imagination.

It always happened that one friendship led to another. At dinner, Jack introduced us to one of his longtime customers, a cattle rancher named W. T. Williams. Peter was in heaven. As a child, he was nicknamed Cowboy. He longed to ride horses, rope calves, and work as a cowpoke, which was a world away from public housing in Greenwich. The dream had never left him. He wanted to experience a cattle drive and feel the romance of the Old West.

One morning, W. T. had us out to his ten-thousand-acre ranch outside Twin Falls, just as his ranch hands were beginning preparations to round up cattle in the hills. He invited us to join the cowpokes.

W. T. was an early pioneer and legend in Magic Valley. He claimed that life "out here" was hard. It would either break a man's back or drive him out of his mind trying to survive on dry ground that wasn't irrigated. W. T. had worked hard his whole life to get anything, especially land. Especially water. And after he arrived in Idaho at age twenty-one, he endured droughts, rustlers, floods, and downright meanness because being a cattle rancher was a poker game. Neighbors were ten miles away. There were no unemployment benefits, food stamps, welfare, first responders, or benevolent organizations. All W. T. had was true grit and bank loans.

"We ain't got time to worry about what they're doin' back in Washington, DC," he said. "All we can do is pray for good weather, keep our cows healthy, and keep steaks on the table. But there's one main thing we don't ever forget out here. . . . We're free!"

Now in his seventies, W. T. let his middle-aged sons and five grandsons run the operation he'd started back in 1922.

When it was time to leave, W. T.'s boys showed us the horses we would ride and explained the basics of the cattle drive. The mission was to round up nine hundred head and drive them back into the Sawtooth Mountains. The cattle needed more grass. They needed more fat before winter. With only a few weeks left of walking, I was excited for one last thrill. I loved the smell of horses and to hear them whinny, snort, breathe, and gallop. I liked the feel of a saddle and the sound of leather rubbing against itself while my horse trotted through the brush.

To be a cowgirl had never been a passion of mine, but my horse and saddle fit like a pair of good shoes. Some part of me was born to ride. I inhaled the earthy smells of sagebrush and horse sweat and sat proud on the back of my horse. I was a natural. This came easy.

"Get goin'! Ho! Ya!" rowdy cowboys hollered, whistling and zigzagging on their horses through hundreds of bawling cattle. Clouds of dust blanketed the horizon, and the men inhaled so much of it that they coughed and spit brown juice just like Granddad in the Ozarks.

"Come on! Move 'em out! Let's go! Back up them mountains!"

It was a dream.

A calf bolted away from the herd and ran toward a stand of willows while a wiry cowboy made chase. Peter raced behind a dozen riders, looking happy, excited, and alive, and they took off like a posse toward Cottonwood Canyon. Peter was a big, stocky man, so he rode a giant horse with hooves like skillets. I rode my shiny brown quarter horse in the opposite direction toward Sugarloaf Canyon with another group of cowpokes in search of stragglers.

My partners on horseback were Charlotte Crockett, Carol Hopwood, and two men whose names I don't remember. Charlotte and Carol were horse lovers and real cowgirls. Charlotte was a short tank of a woman in her late fifties, a widow who ran her own ranch and carried a loaded rifle like a city girl carries a handbag. She remarked that she didn't understand "women's lib" or all the talk about feminism; she considered herself a liberated woman far before feminism was ever invented. She was fascinating to me. Her short gray hair peeked from underneath a cowboy hat as she swung her rope in the air, whistling and hollering at runaway cows. She was far better than most of the men.

Carol was a newlywed in her twenties and from the new generation of cowgirls. Her husband, Rodney, was in the posse of men headed to Cottonwood Canyon with Peter. Her riding skills were smooth as she worked the reins and shouted at stray cows, long dark hair flying behind her, dirt in the corners of her eyes. She and her horse spoke a special language. With the slightest move, he knew just what to do. They were gifted dancers on the open range; they made it look easy.

We rode for eight long hours and rounded up two hundred head of stragglers and their calves. Charlotte and Carol didn't look any worse for wear, but I had swallowed a pint of dust and was covered from head to toe in a brown powder. I felt "rode hard" and exhausted. When we stopped to rest the horses and eat a peanut butter sandwich, I eased my sore backside over to the campfire. My horse stared up at me, chomping on dead grass and looking bored.

"Here," Carol smiled, handing me a tin can full of cowboy coffee. She had boiled it over the campfire, and it was thick, black, and strong enough to jolt a wild stallion and keep a woman in the saddle six more hours. I'd thought we were finished, but on we went.

By the end of the day my nostrils were clogged with so much dirt I could barely breathe, and my butt felt like mashed hamburger meat. I had bounced on the back of a quarter horse for fourteen hours and now knew why all cowboys were so thin and had skinny butts. I wanted to get off and not move for at least a week. When I dismounted, my legs were so bowed, I worried they would never straighten out, and my knees were grinding bone on bone. Charlotte and Carol had unknowingly taught me what it meant to ride hard and hang tough. What a silly fool I had been to think I was a natural cowgirl born to ride. I finally understood the bumper sticker on Carol's truck: "Only Cowgirls Are Brave Enough to Marry Cowboys!"

Back on the ranch, Viola Williams was busy in her kitchen. She was a tiny woman, not five feet tall, with a voice high and sweet. At age seventy-two, she possessed a spirit as frisky as a filly's. She wore her dark hair pulled back in a French roll, and her eyes sparkled against pink-white skin. She reminded me of my Grandma Pennell, whose name was also Viola, and insisted I call her by her first name instead of Mrs. Williams; it felt awkward, but I complied.

"Yes, ma'am."

"Folks said we was lucky," she said, looking back on her own history. "Fifty years ago, we started out as sheepherders and lived in a log cabin."

She pointed across the horizon and said they owned all of it, all the way to the Sawtooth Mountains.

"I've spent the last fifty years takin' care of my boys, cookin' three square meals a day so they could put in a good day's work."

I learned that hard work was a high calling in these parts. Almost like being called to preach the gospel. Viola handled cooking and feeding her men, holy in her own right. She managed everything including the housekeeping because she didn't like other people in her territory. She was happiest when she stood over pots on the stove, manning the phone and CB radio. She was the official dispatcher, like an air traffic controller, and she directed cowpokes where to round up cattle, where to harvest corn, who was accounted for, and who wasn't. From her modest kitchen, Viola handed out assignments like a commander and kept tabs on all things great and small on the four-generation outfit that was worth millions of dollars. *And* she had a reputation as the best cook in Magic Valley.

Her enormous round, laminated table seated ten and was permanently set for anyone who came through the door. The milkman managed to deliver milk at lunchtime so he could join the community table, and Viola's greatest satisfaction came when ranch hands and guests ate hearty and filled their plates two or three times. After the drive, Peter and I were glad to oblige. Every man and animal worked hard on the Williams Ranch, and each person did what they were best cut out for without conformity. Viola considered her role as cook, homemaker, and dispatcher just as important as the cattle work. She did not view herself as second class or less-than. It didn't bother her that she didn't have a title as a manager or executive officer. Young women my age were determined to break the glass ceiling. Viola worked for half a century without noticing it was there.

She gave me a gift she didn't know she'd given and I didn't know I'd needed. From the time I left New Orleans on foot back in July 1976, people had snickered, talked behind my back, and called me crazy.

"There's no way I'd walk across America or carry that heavy backpack, not for love nor money!"

"Aren't you afraid something awful will happen?"

"Don't you worry about getting robbed or killed?"

This little seventy-two-year-old woman bent over her stove and made no apologies or excuses for who she was or what she did. Her actions cleared the fog inside of me. I remembered back in the Ozarks how I cooked, washed clothes in the old wringer washer, ironed clothes, and mopped floors, desperate to do something that "mattered." For the last three years, I had lived like a nomad and slept in a tent. Viola Williams didn't need applause or a stamp of approval to determine her worth, and dear God, I didn't either. Viola knew her cooking, scrubbing, and feeding her boys was an integral part in a bigger picture. I knew I was a part of something bigger, too, and today I felt it.

TWENTY-FOUR

YEARBOOK QUEEN

School of the Ozarks, 1967

During my sophomore year in college, I was assigned the job of campus photographer and to work in the photography lab. It was exciting because it allowed me to express my creativity in photos of people, places, and college life. I spent all my nights with Pat, Lydia, and Steph, listening to "Unchained Melody," talking about boys, smoking, and snapping pictures of dorm life.

As a school photographer. I took hundreds of black-and-white photos for the college newspaper, brochures, and marketing publications, and I learned to develop film and print photos in a dark lab that mostly smelled like chemicals. Little did I know how important a camera and photography would become to my future.

Life on campus was busy with my jobs, classes, and exams. I didn't have much room to date, but once I saw Bruce Jackson, I vowed to make the time. The only problem was that he was going steady with someone else, and she was drop-dead gorgeous.

I found out Bruce was active in student organizations, so I joined every campus activity that would have me, hoping we would cross paths. We didn't. So I thought entering some contests might help. I competed for Homecoming Queen, Yearbook Queen, "Best Dressed," and more. I had no illusions about winning, especially as queen of anything. No one had ever told me I was pretty except Uncle Glenn, and Mother told him to shut his mouth.

Some of the competitions required evening gowns, and I hesitated to ask Mother to make them. She was an excellent seamstress but worried about the cost of the fabric. After assuring Mother I could buy the fabric from my wages cleaning houses, she finally agreed and made the most beautiful gowns for me. One was pink chiffon and one was gold satin, and they were floor-length and sleeveless with a scooped neckline, fitted at the waist. They shimmered under the light. I had no way of knowing if they made me look beautiful, but I imagined I was a princess in them. I felt transformed from a hillbilly into Cinderella. Because of the thick wall between Mother and me, she couldn't wish me well, tell me I looked pretty, or say she hoped I would win. Instead, she showed me her love and support the best way a hillbilly can: sweat equity. To my total and absolute surprise, I won Yearbook Queen.

"How does it feel to be the prettiest girl on campus?" one boy asked. I was dumbfounded.

———

Shortly after, Bruce Jackson started to come into the library more often, and we had brief exchanges whenever he checked out a book. He never mentioned what caused the breakup between him and his beautiful girlfriend, who no doubt should have been the

Yearbook Queen. Once we started dating, it didn't matter. We were together every free moment until he graduated. He was two years ahead of me, and after school was out, he gave me an engagement ring. I was the happiest hillbilly girl in all the Ozarks. That is, until he joined the Army and was deployed to Korea.

———————

After graduating from college, I started working for the Department of Welfare while my handsome fiancé served across the world. I stayed busy as a social worker helping poor hillbillies and descendants of sharecroppers access government services. Some people thought I was uppity because I had a college degree. Who did I think I was "risin' above my raisins"?

I didn't care. It was important for me to appear professional and do my job, even when I wanted to remind people that I had come from the same kind of places they had. I dressed in skirts and stockings and quit smoking cigarettes. The hillbilly women I knew had deep, raspy voices and faces covered in wrinkles from a lifetime of smoking Lucky Strikes. I worried I was staring into my future. Pride told me to lay down the tobacco.

I missed my fiancé horribly. He was on another continent, and I felt displaced; it was lonely. I wanted to enjoy my life—I was hardly the only girl with a man away in the military—but I was haunted by Mother's accusations that I was fickle, so I was hesitant when friends invited me to parties or dance clubs. Mother's words rang loudly in my head. What if I couldn't trust myself? What if I were just a flirt and weak? As the love letters from my fiancé slipped to the back of my mind, I broke down and joined friends for evenings out. Handsome guys bought me beers and invited me to dance.

They thought I was pretty. At first, I declined, but then I told myself, "What could it hurt?" There was no harm in having a good time. It felt so good to laugh and flirt and feel a man's arms around me. Naive and unguarded, it wasn't long before I cheated on the man I had worked so hard to get. The man to whom I was engaged.

When Bruce finished his overseas tour, he returned home and was thrilled to see me. But his heart was broken in pieces when I returned his engagement ring. I didn't know how to tell him the truth: that I had been unfaithful and was full of guilt and shame. He was a good and honorable man who loved me and didn't deserve my infidelity.

I never wanted any part of being double-minded or fickle. I prayed it wouldn't come back to hurt me like the Bible says: "Be not deceived; God is not mocked: for whatsoever a man soweth, that shall he also reap" (Galatians 6:7 KJV).

Once I asked God to forgive me, and after I finally forgave myself, I made loyalty a badge of honor for the rest of my life.

TWENTY-FIVE

THE COLDEST WINTER SINCE 1919

Idaho, November 1978

We crossed into Oregon along the railroad tracks. I watched my feet as we carefully walked across a railroad trestle high over the Snake River, and the wind was so strong and cold that it took my breath away. The sky was gray and gloomy, and I knew winter was at our heels. Every step was dangerous and a push into the biting wind. Peter and I strained to listen for a train whistle and prayed to make it across before a locomotive rounded the bend. There were no guardrails on the trestle that spanned one side of the river to the other, and when I looked down, I felt dizzy. If either of us fell into the river, we would be swept away. We were weary twentieth-century pioneers motivated to press on.

When my feet touched the same ruts made by wagon trains on the Oregon Trail, I drew strength from the earth and knew each step brought me closer to the end of the walk and to the Pacific

Ocean. I had gained a deeper understanding of my country, one step at a time, and a new awareness of my own hillbilly history, strengths, motivations, and who I was and who I wasn't. On the edge of Ontario, we saw a sign ahead that said, "Where Oregon Begins."

Ontario was a small multicultural town along the Snake River and the Oregon–Idaho border. The area was rugged in parts but prime land for growing onions, potatoes, beets, and most of the world's zinnia seeds. We were told Ontario had the highest Japanese American population per capita in the state, possibly because internment camps had existed nearby in the 1940s. Migrant farmworkers also came to the region to help with the agricultural demands. This part of Oregon was diverse, productive, and clean. There was no trash along the road—or anywhere, for that matter.

Because of its volcanoes, Oregon was one of the most geographically unique states in the country. It had rich soil, abundant water, evergreen and mixed forests, high deserts, and semi-arid shrub lands. But most importantly, Oregon was the last state we had to walk across before reaching the Pacific Ocean.

As soon as we crossed the border, I could tell something was wrong with me. I felt weak and sick as we plodded along two-lane Highway 26. We were in the state less than a week before I needed to stop. I was terribly ill. This was different from heat stroke or soreness after riding a horse all day. I was rarely sick on the road, but my back and neck ached, and my stomach was upset. I also had diarrhea. We always ate whatever food we could get in a store, café, gas station, or someone's home, because we never knew when we would eat next. I reasoned that it had to be food poisoning. We stopped and stayed in a cheap motel for a few days because I was weak and couldn't keep anything down. Then I told myself I felt better, to ignore feeling sick and keep walking, so we walked eleven miles to Willow Creek. It was wrenching for a few days, and later I felt better.

———————

The weather turned bitter cold, and by the time we walked into Brogan, Oregon, on November 15, 1978, it was two degrees and snowing. This was the first snowfall of the year, and although we knew we'd face bad weather ahead, we were like horses headed to the barn. Short of being kidnapped by aliens or run over by an eighteen-wheeler, nothing could stop us now. We were less than four hundred miles from the end of our three-thousand mile walk from New Orleans to the Pacific Ocean.

Peter walked twenty paces ahead as we moved slowly west across windswept plains and a lonely highway that disappeared over the horizon. Cattle huddled together on the range for protection from the high winds, snow, and freezing rain. It was twenty-eight degrees the day we made it to Ironside, population thirty-seven. A rural mail carrier and his wife, Lawrence and Trudy McCracken, stopped to talk to us in the sparsely populated Malheur County. They had read about us on the front page of *The Argus Observer*, the regional newspaper since 1897. The couple brought us hot coffee and food and treated us like we were long-lost relatives. The mailman said we would never know what meeting us had done for them.

I didn't understand why we were so important to people, but we had interactions like this over and over. America was fascinated by us. Maybe it was because they read about us or saw us on television or because we were nonthreatening and approachable on foot. Maybe they were disillusioned like Peter or fulfilling a calling like me. Everyone wanted to help us, even when they thought we were out of our minds. To some, we symbolized travel and adventure they couldn't find in their own lives, or we reminded them of their youth. To others, perhaps we embodied hopes and dreams for the future or reminded them of a distant son or daughter. A few said we illustrated the heart and soul of America. I didn't know about all that. If people had known how flawed and dysfunctional we were as a couple, no one would have been impressed. Our marriage was fire and water, yin and yang. We were contrary forces that complemented each other, and no matter how much I prayed or tried, we couldn't seem to reach a comfortable balance.

"Thank you for the coffee and letting us warm up in your car," I said to the mailman and his wife as we shook hands and stepped back into the cold. "It was nice to meet you." The old mail carrier had tears in his eyes.

"God bless you, Mr. McCracken," I added as we waved goodbye.

"He already has," he said before driving away.

I was deeply touched but couldn't allow myself to shed a tear because I had miles to walk. Crying took energy I needed for the road.

Clouds hung low, and the sky looked like it was going to dump a foot of snow the entire nineteen miles we walked toward Unity, Oregon. In this small town with less than a hundred people, we found a cheap motel to get warm, have a meal, rest up, and take a hot bath. We also wanted to watch the weather report on television because we were headed into the Cascade Mountains. Channel 6 flashed "Breaking News" across the screen. They were forecasting the biggest blizzard of the year. It had already dropped four inches of snow in Portland, and travel advisories were issued across the entire Northwest and the Cascades. The forecast was much worse than either of us could have imagined, but we couldn't hole up for an entire season. The weatherman said it would be the coldest winter since 1919, and we were headed straight into it, ready or not.

We walked toward the mountains all the next day in thick falling snow. I kept my head down to shield my face from the giant, white flakes. My hands and feet were frozen stubs, and I couldn't feel my toes. Everything in sight was covered in white as we trudged along Highway 26. We heard nothing except the crunch of snow under our boots. I tried to think of other things besides my frozen limbs, so I imagined tables of Southern food and remembered the warmer states we had walked across: Louisiana, Texas, Colorado, New Mexico, Utah, and Idaho. We were eight miles out of John Day, Oregon, our next stop, a town of two thousand people with the Strawberry Mountains to the south and the Blue Mountains to the east. We were less than three hundred miles to the Pacific Ocean.

At this moment, nothing mattered except finding shelter where we could get warm. I was worried. My down jacket and hood kept my head and torso warm, but my eyes and nose were exposed, and the tip of my nose was as red as Rudolph's.

Peter had disappeared ahead in thick sheets of snow, and I was alone in a silent world. I wanted to stop and sit on a rock because I was so cold and tired, and I imagined how wonderful it would be to rest, lie down, and drift off to sleep. I was pondering the comfort of sleep when I heard a crack. It sounded like someone had stepped on a branch. Was another person out here in this blizzard? White flurries filled the air and blocked my vision. I had to blink several times and squint to keep snow out of my eyes before I saw it. There, a few feet in front of me, stood a fawn with big brown eyes and a cape of snow on its back—seemingly amazed to see a human being. The fawn belonged here, and we both knew that I didn't.

I don't know whether it was the big hump on my back or the fact that my face was covered in a hoodie, but I didn't seem to frighten the beautiful young animal. We stood in silent whiteness and observed each other when warm thoughts came to my mind, as if an angel in the form of a fawn infused me with words such as "do not be afraid; the town of John Day is near." Before the fawn faded into a fog of snow, he looked back at me with the kindest eyes and a pledge: "You will be alright."

I rounded a snowbank and brushed the snow out of my eyes. Then Peter came into view. His head was down and pointed into strong gusts of wind, so he had no idea what I had seen or why I suddenly found the strength to walk a little faster. Help was on the way.

———

Christmas 1978 proved to be unlike any I had ever experienced in my hillbilly childhood or anywhere in the South. Shortly after my encounter with the angelic fawn in the snowstorm, a car appeared on the empty road. The driver was Mary Lou Koto, who had heard we were headed into her town. Of course, newspapers were filled with gossip about the crazy hikers, tall tales swirling like the Oregon blizzard. Mary Lou was determined to find us. She brought hot chocolate and told us a local church ahead was waiting to help. And, by the way, would we like to spend Christmas Day with her and her husband and his mother? I never would have imagined spending Christmas in the home of a Japanese American family. If there were Japanese Americans in the Ozarks, I'd never seen or met them. Of course, we took her up on the invitation.

On December 25, 1978, Tish Koto, a kind, silver-haired woman, sat on the floor and lovingly washed and rubbed my road-weary feet. She spoke quietly and graciously answered a string of questions about her life. I sensed she was holding emotions in check as she explained how her parents were forced into Minidoka Relocation Center at Hunt, Idaho. Some of the camps were prisons with deplorable living conditions, surrounded by barbed wire and guard towers. I was mesmerized by her life story.

I wasn't a huge history buff and didn't know that after Japan bombed Pearl Harbor, the American newspapers printed headlines like, "The Japanese May Try Anything." People like Tish and her relatives were considered "enemy aliens" and prohibited from owning firearms, explosives, shortwave radios, and cameras. The American government froze Japanese bank assets and imposed travel restrictions and a curfew. On February 19, 1942, President Franklin D. Roosevelt said, "The Japanese race is an enemy race," and ordered all people of Japanese ancestry to be moved inland from the West Coast. Their businesses, homes, and property were sold at whatever price they could get, and it wasn't until January 1945 that Tish and her family were free to leave the camp.

After they were released, Tish married Masato Koto, and they had one child. Mike Koto was a third-generation Japanese man born in the United States and called *sansei*. He became the center of the Koto family's hopes and dreams for the future. Mike and I were close in age and part of the new generation far removed from the war. From that war, anyway.

Tish prayed for a better life for her son, that he would be free from accusations and prejudices she had faced. But she warned him, "You must not get into trouble or do anything wrong. People will always remember because you look different on the outside. If other people do wrong, it is forgotten. But if you do wrong, my son, you must not bring any shame to your grandparents or to our family name."

With Tish at my feet, how could I not mull over unfair prejudices that had been a plague throughout history? I was steeped in hillbilly culture, which came with preconceptions of its own. Hillbillies were suspicious of anyone different. It was assumed educated people were snobs and wealthy people were born with a silver spoon in their mouths, and hard-working people had no time for lazy, good-for-nothing folks. Hillbillies were wary of anyone who wasn't poor and held no respect for black people on welfare, even though most folks on my street accepted the same government food commodities. We passed our misconceptions from one generation to another, which left most of us terribly biased.

Listening to Tish, it was clear that misunderstandings and misjudgments traveled far beyond the Ozark hills. The racial prejudice, war hysteria, and failure of political leadership left Japanese American families with shame, humiliation, and lifelong scars.

Tish's foot massage helped me relax and eased the nausea I felt. I didn't know why my stomach was so upset and I hoped it wouldn't interfere with her Christmas meal. The fire popped in the wood stove, and I soaked up its warmth from the sofa. This moment was locked in time and seemed surreal. The sweet aging woman at my feet had lived a life totally different from mine. Tish had experienced abuse and tyranny, and I wondered how she had resolved the injustice in her own mind. She did not exhibit anger or bitterness but rather a demeanor of kindness and gratitude. Tish embodied forgiveness, and I was a poor hillbilly from the wrong side of the tracks still trying to escape the prejudices from my upbringing and still kicking against everything unfair. I felt like I had experienced the whole world on our walk but still knew nothing.

I pondered the meaning of freedom and how it tolls. Every generation has cried and prayed for it. Men and women have fought and died for it. It was for freedom that Moses led slaves out of Egypt, and it was for freedom and justice that Martin Luther King Jr. led black folk from Selma to Montgomery. Would humankind ever find the way to freedom and justice on this earth?

All day long, the Koto house filled with the smells of food and fresh pine. Mike and Mary Lou Koto were excited we had joined them. Their family tradition consisted of a Japanese meal prepared by Mike's mother: nori sushi, aburage, mazegohan, shrimp tempura, and yokan dessert. Tish had driven six hours from Twin Falls to John Day to cook and spend the day with her kids, while it took Peter and me two and a half years to get here on foot.

Mary Lou made stockings for all of us. Five of them hung behind the wood-burning stove as we gathered around their decorated tree. Mike played Santa Claus, while Tish glowed with joy in our midst. She was happy to be with her son and daughter-in-law and their newfound friends. The snow fell softly outside and became a perfect setting as we laughed, talked, and opened gifts. Mike gave us a brass plaque in the shape of Oregon with this inscription: Peter and Barbara Jenkins, A Walk Across America, Alfred, New York, October 15, 1973–Florence, Oregon, January 18, 1979, 4,800 miles.

We gave Tish an inexpensive crystal dish we had bought the day before when she said she would never buy anything so fancy for herself. I gave Mary Lou a handpicked bouquet of wild herbs in a basket with a ribbon tied around it. Peter gave Mike an electric iron because he and Mary Lou mentioned needing one to press their clothes. Tish gave us hand warmers. Boy, would we need them. The last present under the tree was for Peter, a blue cotton T-shirt with bold letters: "O-R-E-G-U-N"

Mike said, "That's the way we natives pronounce our state."

It was an unforgettable and untouchable Christmas, a landmark of awareness. I had walked out of New Orleans one way, but after staying with real people from Louisiana to Oregon, eating at their tables, sleeping in their beds, and hearing their life stories, I had changed. I wasn't the same person. So many fears and opinions had melted in my mind like ice in sunshine. It wasn't head knowledge or something out of a book but face-to-face chance meetings with all sorts of people. This was the Christmas that the North Star shined on me. The suffering and kindness of Tish Koto made me realize that the love in her heart and the blood in her veins was the same as mine. We were all travelers—sore, scarred, and blistered, doing the best we knew how.

TWENTY-SIX

CASCADES AHEAD

Oregon, January 1979

It was brutally cold when we got back on the road and headed west into the Cascades. We walked on Highway 26 across the Ring of Fire, the area in the Pacific Cascadia Range notorious for volcanic eruptions. Lewis and Clark had called them the "Western Mountains." I'd heard of Mount Rainier, Mount Adams, Mount Hood, and Mount Saint Helens, but I had never heard of "Three Sisters," peaks, discovered in 1854, that rose side by side more than ten thousand feet. Early pioneers named them Faith, Hope, and Charity.

During the summer months, the Cascades were full of alpine meadows, waterfalls, lava fields, canyons, and lakes, but during the final days of our walk across America, all we saw was a frozen expanse and blowing snow. We lowered our heads and pushed into winds that whipped like sharp leather straps. The last week of December 1978 was fierce. We trudged ahead, exhausted and afraid to stop for fear we might freeze in place.

Thomas Fuller was an English historian and the first to claim that "the darkest hour was just before the dawn." We had no idea when the darkest hour was because, in the Cascades, they all felt bleak. The only hint of light across the killer Cascades was one man named Milo. He was unlike anyone I had ever met.

Milo Franke was a seventy-year-old rancher, logger, and cowboy turned mountain preacher. He served as pastor of the Assembly of God Church in John Day, and everyone in the small town knew him as Brother Milo. Tall and angular, he dressed like Johnny Cash in a long, split-tail black coat and cowboy boots. Under a wide-brimmed cowboy hat, he sported thick, gray hair and bushy, lambchop sideburns stretching all the way down to his jawline. His glacier-blue eyes seemed sharp enough to split wood. With the presence and power of a bar room bouncer (or a biblical prophet), Milo was nobody's fool, and he didn't play games. He was authentic from his cowboy hat down to his cowboy boots.

Milo rode a horse throughout the high country to preach to loggers and miners; in town, he would park his motorcycle in front of saloons and bring the good news to lonely men as they drowned their sorrows in shots of whisky. He claimed riding horses and motorcycles was cheaper than buying gas. Milo was a man who didn't cower from uncomfortable situations; instead, he charged into them like a bull and dared a weak man to face the demons inside his soul. He became a laser light in dark places, and his war cry was "Glory to God!"

Back in John Day, Mike and Mary Lou Koto had taken us to meet Brother Milo at a midweek church service. After one look at Peter and me, Milo announced we would perish crossing the Cascades without help, so he stood in front of his small and faithful congregation and asked permission to take off a week to follow us in his car while we walked across the mountains. The congregation applauded and agreed it was God's will for him to help us.

So there we were, walking on a 107-mile stretch through the Ochoco Mountains toward Prineville on ice-packed roads bordered by deep snowbanks. Strong headwinds pushed against us. Ponderosa pine, juniper, layers of lava, prehistoric fossils, and all the earth lay buried under a thick blanket of white. Prineville was only forty-seven miles southwest, but I wasn't sure if I could make it. It was two below zero during the day and twenty-five below at night. I had also started to feel terribly sick again. I ached all over, and my head and chest hurt. I was nauseated and worried it was an early sign of pneumonia. Mother told me I had pneumonia a few times as a child and that my lungs were susceptible. The pain and worry were so extreme, I held back tears. I would have let go but was afraid my tears would freeze on my face. I forced myself to keep walking for Peter's sake, for my sake, for God's sake, and for *National Geographic*. I was dangerously drained, but I put one foot in front of the other. Peter worried we might not make the last two hundred miles, and if we didn't, it would be my fault.

Milo knew the Cascade Mountains could destroy a person's will and defeat even the toughest outdoorsman, so he drove at two miles per hour in an old sedan next to me, giving me hot coffee and cocoa to keep me from freezing. When the winds became so strong we couldn't walk, Peter and I sat in Milo's car to thaw and eat whatever he'd brought. One afternoon when we crawled out of the car, Milo saw how sick I was and told Peter there was something wrong with me. He was right, and I was glad he had spoken up. I needed to see a doctor, and Peter agreed. He knew something was wrong but didn't know how to help me.

———————

"I got a longtime friend who's a doctor in Prineville. His name is Dr. Elon Wood, and I know he'll see Barbara," Milo said.

I believed Peter was more worried than he let on, and I know it worried me.

It was January 2, 1979, when Milo drove Peter and me over the icy roads to Dr. Wood's office. My imagination went wild. I wondered if I had a severe case of the flu or something more daunting like leukemia or maybe a rare blood disease. I had never been this depleted in my life, and I'd heard people with terminal illnesses were extremely tired. I understood what it felt like to be sick from drinking out of a drainage ditch or tired from walking twenty miles in boiling sun, but this was different. Peter and Milo waited outside the exam room while a nurse asked me questions, wrote down information, and drew blood.

When Dr. Wood finally walked back in the room, he was stone-faced, devoid of any emotion.

Why do doctors unfailingly look like mannequins when they deliver their patients' results?

My heartbeat was so fast I could hear it thumping in my chest. He looked in my eyes and said the tests revealed two important things I needed to know.

Oh, dear God, what?

I knew it was going to be bad.

Here it comes.

My heart sank at the thought of having to go into a hospital or not finishing our walk across America, because we were so close to the end.

"Did you know that you could sell your blood?" he asked casually. His question took me by complete surprise; I had no idea what he was talking about.

"Only 2 percent of the population in the entire world has your blood type," he explained.

I never cared about my blood type, and what difference would it make if I was going to *die*? I held my breath and waited through several agonizing seconds before he told me the next thing I needed to know.

"Mrs. Jenkins, the blood tests revealed you have B negative blood," he said. "And that you are six weeks pregnant and should deliver in mid-August."

I was so stunned I didn't know what to say. My mouth dropped open, and nothing came out until I caught my breath.

"Are you kidding me?" I stammered.

Emotion filled my body in an avalanche; I was shocked, thrilled, happy, afraid, excited, and anxious all at once. I had so many feelings and questions.

Was it too dangerous to walk pregnant in Arctic temperatures?

What if I had a miscarriage? What if I lost the baby due to the extreme conditions?

Would a baby heal my marriage?

Would it make Peter less angry? Would it make me less of a pushover?

What if? What if? What if?

Dr. Wood listened to my medical questions and assured me I was young, strong, and healthy. Because Milo was going to follow us through the mountain passes, there was no reason I couldn't walk the last two hundred miles to finish the walk across America. It was the kind of thing only a mountain doctor in the Cascades would approve of. He said that once we were beyond Santiam Pass, the climate would be warmer because we would enter the coastal range.

In a stupor, I followed the doctor to the crowded lobby. Peter and Milo waited anxiously and were on the edges of their seats when we entered the room. Dr. Wood reported that I was perfectly fine, nothing serious, and that I was a month and a half pregnant. Peter and Milo erupted into yelps and loud cheers. Peter grabbed and kissed me while Milo whooped his war cry, "Glory to God!" Everyone in the waiting room smiled and enjoyed the happy diversion from the gray day of falling snow.

Dr. Wood also explained that I had the RH negative factor, which would be of concern if the baby was RH positive. If our incompatible blood mixed, it could harm the baby. I was too nauseated to comprehend what he was talking about. Within the hour, I had learned I had a rare blood type, was pregnant, and was RH negative. To top it off, I had two hundred miles to walk before I reached the Pacific Coast. I was a young woman who didn't care about anything except to keep from vomiting in front of a lobby full of strangers. Peter's face flushed with excitement, and he was euphoric knowing he was going to be a father.

The next day was my darkest hour before the dawn. Milo dropped us back on the highway where we had stopped before going to see

Dr. Wood, and the weather, impossibly, was worse. Milo followed along beside me at a turtle's pace as we inched slowly through another day of unrelenting snow and icy winds. This was the kind of weather that knocked out power lines and downed trees and caused a foolish and unprepared outdoorsman to end up with frostbite, hypothermia, or dead. Here I was, on the road in the middle of Oregon, exposed to winter's vengeance, sick as a dog, and pregnant.

I leaned into blowing snow and kept my head down to avoid stinging barbs of snow mixed with sleet. The visibility was so low that it was hard to see Peter ahead, but I pushed one foot in front of the other to keep going. Milo saw how pale and nauseous I was, and when a logging truck passed and threw snow in my face, he cranked up the heat in his car as high as it would go and told me to walk next to his open window.

The old preacher's dogged persistence prodded me to keep going. His enthusiasm never wavered as he cheered, quoted Bible verses, and one time stopped the car, jumped out, and rolled in the snow to make me laugh. I forced a smile, but nothing could hide how drained of energy I was. I wanted to drop in my tracks to end the misery. Surely God heard my cries and would do something before I fainted. Oh, God, help me or I will surely die! There was no doubt Milo Franke was my handpicked guardian angel. Not everyone ends up with a rugged logger-rancher-miner-preacher to guide, protect, and goad them to keep going, shouting "Glory to God!" every other breath and staring down the devil underneath the blankets of snow. But I needed a miracle or at least some kind of sign.

"God's gonna get you through to the other side, Barbara!" he shouted.

"Yeah, sure thing," I said.

I hoped he was right but didn't have the strength to believe a word he said.

Suddenly, the strong headwinds stopped, and an eerie, muted silence fell across the forest and road. It was like being in the eye of a hurricane. Everything was still. The ponderosa pines had transformed into a sea of Christmas trees with branches laden in heavy clumps of white. Milo popped in an old gospel tape and turned the volume to maximum, and the music sounded like we were in a recording studio or cozy chapel. The world of snow absorbed the sounds of music. Any other time, I would have preferred the Bee Gees' "You and me, girl, we got a highway to the sky," but at this moment I was glad to be alive, to feel my fingers and toes, and to hear Milo's gospel music. It sounded like heaven on earth.

"Come on!" Milo shouted. "Come on, Barbara, baby! You walk, and I'll throw up!"

I laughed out loud at how ridiculous he was, and Milo grinned from ear to ear because he knew his antics were working. He was doing what Peter couldn't in these circumstances. Milo was saving my life.

"Whoop-ee!" he shouted above the gospel music. "Glory to God!"

TWENTY-SEVEN

SEMINARY

New Orleans, 1975

I was twenty-seven years old when I enrolled in seminary to pursue a master's degree in religious education. I enjoyed working at the Department of Welfare, doing social work in the Ozarks, and serving the people I grew up with. For two years, I spent my days helping poor hillbilly families with children access the provisions and government services to which they were entitled, all while they stared me down with their hopeless and beaten-down eyes, trapped in generational poverty and wondering if I thought I was better than they were. I'd worked my whole life to get away from South Eleventh Street and the roadblocks to a better life. But I needed something more than social work. I ventured that maybe God would guide me.

New Orleans was home to the New Orleans Baptist Theological Seminary and a city drenched in mysticism, jazz, vice, Catholicism, liquor, and the lore of the bayou. I didn't know what I would do with a master's degree in religion, but the idea of the Dead Sea

Scrolls and ancient scriptural texts energized me and sparked my curiosity. I had a starving, curious nature; loved history, religion, and adventure; and wanted to know about the world beyond the Ozarks. And then the world beyond that one and on and on.

Unlike other women on campus, I wasn't pious or looking to become a preacher's wife. I simply liked Psalms and Proverbs, studying the Old and New Testaments, and reading about Middle Eastern cultures. Chasing men wasn't on my mind either, which was good because seminary was hardly the place for dating. When female students entered a classroom, they received lingering side glances but nothing more. Most of the men were married and focused on their doctoral programs and preaching skills, and the few single men struggled to stay spiritually minded. I watched it all, taking notes in the classrooms.

———————

My roommate in William Carey Hall was a dependable, quiet, and witty young woman named Ann Green. She was petite, with brown hair, hazel eyes, and a contagious laugh. Level-headed and thoughtful, she seemed a perfect candidate for the role of preacher's wife, unlike me. Ann and I became fast friends. She experienced God in her quiet manner while I charged ahead with challenging questions—a live wire, highly adventurous and ready for a good time at a moment's notice. I wasn't going to find God in an orderly religious institution; I was going to chase Him down out there somewhere.

Despite our differences, Ann and I balanced each other's personalities and temperaments and I rarely attended class or chapel without her. More than a few times, we took off downtown for shrimp po' boys and a drive through the Garden District in my red VW Beetle, driving past stately homes and lush parks dotted with giant live oaks. She needed my spunky enthusiasm, and I needed her steady hand. Though I never told her, the safety of our bond gave me the courage to face wounds from my childhood I'd been carrying my whole life.

———

Some of my warmest childhood memories had been in South Poplar Bluff General Baptist Church. The smell of the old hymnals and the sound of Laverne Eaker's alto were stitched into my soul, but I felt I had much to learn about God, Christianity, and the human spirit. I was dogged in my faith, so at seminary I wasn't afraid to test other beliefs, criticize institutional religion, or explore. I wrote term papers such as "God Can Handle Your Questions" and attended varieties of worship services from Jewish synagogues to Charismatic temples. I was making straight A's and producing some excellent scholastic papers, but I wasn't satisfied. Some days, I felt I needed to witness a miracle to really be in touch with the Almighty, something like Charlton Heston's parting of the Red Sea in *The Ten Commandments*. The closest I'd ever come was jumping off the smoke house with an umbrella at ten years old and not breaking my legs. (I was hoping I could fly.)

In those days, the passionate and visionary young men on campus, most of whom came from the South, were trained to be polished preachers with three-point sermons that ended in an altar call. The more I listened to them practice their sermons, the more predictable they became. They would not be the deliverers of the miraculous that I sought. In fact, they were so dull, I often dozed off. I counted myself lucky if I didn't fall asleep, bored out of my mind. Seminary wasn't going to be the answer for me. I didn't know what was. I wanted to feel something, and although I liked to have fun, I wasn't interested in drugs, drinking, or casual sex.

Still a hillbilly in my soul, young, naive, and daring, I was blinded by my imagination and unrealistic expectations. Mother always said my eyes were bigger than my belly, which meant a lot of things. I hated to admit she was right.

TWENTY-EIGHT

ONE MORE MILE

Florence, Oregon, January 1979

We finally made it beyond the whiteouts, blizzards, and freezing winds to a dirty slush on the side of the highway. It was January 4, 1979. The temperature had become a balmy thirty degrees, and we started to sweat in our goose-down wilderness coats. With the worst winter since 1919 behind us, Milo knew he had completed his assigned mission.

He hugged Peter and me and gave us his blessing. Then he turned his old car around and drove back down the perilous stretches of road back home to his loving wife, Evelyn, and the faithful flock who had prayed for our safe passage across the Cascades.

Peter and I were like homing pigeons. We walked west, closer to the sea and setting sun. I carried my heavy backpack and new life inside my body, still feeling nauseous and ready for respite. *Dear Lord, we were so near!* Less than a hundred miles from the end of our almost three-year adventure. I knew it was unlikely, but I was sure I could smell the Pacific Ocean.

We slowly approached a community called Blue River, and the landscape changed from barren, windswept rock to misty and lush green. Even on foot, it was dramatic. The subzero gusts had turned into chilly, moist breezes, and the white world we had walked through was now a jungle of ferns, thick grasses, and forest. We were on Oregon Route 126 in the Willamette National Forest walking alongside a meandering river looking like melted sapphires. No wonder someone had named the tiny town Blue River. I had never seen a river *so* blue.

We had to figure out some logistics before we splashed into the ocean, because we planned to invite family, friends, and supporters to walk the last mile of the way with us. Organizing an event was complicated since we were on the road without access to an office, fax machine, phone, or money. We wanted to invite people from New York, Connecticut, North Carolina, Louisiana, Texas, Missouri, Colorado, and everywhere we walked in between.

We were told weather on the Oregon coast was unpredictable and usually cold and rainy in January. Also, we had to consider the conditions across the entire country, because people would have to make travel arrangements from all corners of America. Peter's parents needed a full week to drive from Connecticut. Others would fly. Although my Ozarks parents had traveled to California in an old motor home, they had never flown in an airplane and were not about to start now. They were finicky about drinking water and carried gallon jugs of their own water everywhere they went. Daddy called a glass of water from his Ozark tap a "well house high ball." To them, water from the Ozarks was the best and cleanest water on earth. And if it wasn't the best, they wouldn't drink it.

I was excited to see family, but I had no idea how to go about organizing something of this magnitude.

Where would people stay?

What about food?

What about a program?

What about . . . *everything*?

The number-one song in the nation in January 1979 was "Le Freak," with its lyrics beginning, "One, two, ah, freak out!" That's exactly how I felt.

Thankfully, with the help of our *National Geographic* editors and our team at William Morrow, we reserved a modest motel called Driftwood Shores near the coast in Florence, Oregon, our final destination. It was sixty miles west of the airport in Eugene and a manageable distance for those who flew into the airport and rented a car. We spoke with the motel manager, Mr. Hager, and he was happy to arrange a fresh seafood buffet for everyone after we ended our well-publicized walk across America. The thought of seafood turned my stomach, but I believed everyone who came would love it.

Once we set the date to end the walk, I created a handwritten invitation and drew a rudimentary map of Oregon. We mailed copies to everyone for whom we had addresses. We weren't sure if anyone would come in the middle of winter except our parents, but we hoped a dozen or more could make it. Here's what my invitation said:

After many years and thousands of miles, we have reached Oregon and are very close to ending our walk in Florence on January 18, 1979. We want to invite you to come join us on this special occasion. Parents, relatives, our pastor (from New Orleans), and people we have met on the walk, *National Geographic*, and even our 83-year-old Grandma will be there. Barbara Jo and Peter

My Grandma Pennell (Daddy's mother) was the only living grandparent between us. She lived in Phoenix, Arizona, and accepted our invitation immediately, promising that her doctor had given her written permission to fly. At age eighty-three, Viola Louise Pennell was going to think positive and not worry about her fragile heart condition. She said, "I've never been to Oregon, but I'll see you there. I'm so thankful to both of you for wanting me to share it with you. I believe God has answered my prayers to protect you."

———————

Finally, the long-awaited day, January 18, arrived. Everything felt surreal and blurry. We had literally walked across America. We had thousands of miles under our feet and now there was only one left. A swell of emotions flooded my heart, along with memories and multiple sights, smells, and sounds, from New Orleans to Oregon. I wanted to savor every second of the grand finale, but the walk had taught us that no matter how victorious, tragic, or historic, time won't stop or slow, it won't be grabbed, trapped, or frozen, not for us or anyone else.

Word of our celebration spread among locals in Florence, and I was shocked to see the large crowd of family, friends, and strangers gathered at 10:00 a.m. sharp at the one-mile marker we'd agreed upon. It was a crisp, chilly morning, and the sun shone bright. Everyone said how unusual it was to see such a clear, sunny day on the Oregon coast during the heart of winter, but it was what I had prayed for.

Among the people gathered to walk the last mile were Don and Sarah Stevens from the Texas Panhandle; M. C. and Ms. Margaret Jenkins from Alabama; our pastor Charles and Barbara Green from New Orleans; Perk and Emma Jean Vickers from Lake City, Colorado; Mary Elizabeth, Eric, and Marguerite from North Carolina (the family Peter stayed with); Jack and Lucy Ramsey from Filer, Idaho; Bill, Viola, and Billy Williams from Twin Falls, Idaho; the Wysockis; Phillip Yancey; old friends from seminary; Harvey Arden, our editor from *National Geographic*; Larry Hughes, president of William Morrow Publishing Company; Pat Golbitz, our book editor; and Joan Stewart, our agent from William Morris. As beautiful as the faces I knew were the ones I had never seen before.

Daddy, Mother, and my sister, Vicky, drove from the Ozarks in an old motor home, and Peter's family rented a car and drove from Connecticut. It was a day of destiny. I looked across the diverse crowd and saw rich and poor, black and white, old and young, urban and rural. These were the people I had come to know, love, and understand because I had crossed amber waves of grain, purple mountain majesties, and the fruited plains, where I had met them, eaten at their tables, and heard their stories. On this day, we were sharing a moment bigger than any one of us. Overhead, a helicopter circled as reporters, photographers, and television videographers surrounded the crowd. Paparazzi circled us and followed along as we walked down to the beach.

Grandma walked between me and Peter while the crowd fell into place behind us. We walked at a slow and leisurely pace for

Grandma's sake while she sang an old hymn she had learned back at Johnston Chapel in the Ozarks, the same country church she took me to when I was a child. Her voice was squeaky and still off-key but also triumphant: "When I've gone the last mile of the way, I will rest at the close of the day, and I know there are joys that await me."

Ahead and above us was a line of sand dunes that hid the great blue waters of the Pacific Ocean. I could smell the sea and hear its roar as waves crashed ashore, like clapping hands applauding us, I reasoned, during our final steps. We had finally reached the end.

Grandma asked to stop as we started up the incline. Her heart had started to flutter, and she needed a nitroglycerin pill. We stopped, halting the train of people as Grandma reached in her coat pocket for her medicine. Once Grandma was ready, we slowly inched our way up the steep dune. The instant we crested the top, my eyes fixed on the biggest and deepest ocean in the world, and it swept my heart away. The water shimmered in the sunshine, and luxurious waves danced toward the shore. It was a wondrous moment, too big for my human body to absorb and too glorious for emotions or trite words. As a girl, I was baptized in an Ozark river, and now I was being christened by the magnificent Pacific Ocean.

———————

When I looked out across the Pacific, everything around me faded. For a fleeting second, I wondered if Mother was proud of me. Had I made my Ozark hillbilly ancestors proud? But nothing mattered now except to reach the sea. The horizon stretched wide open and endless. Our journey had taken almost three years, one step at a time, to reach this spot. Peter dropped Grandma's hand and grabbed mine, and we hurried down the dune toward the beach and billowy waves and into the beautiful water and endless sky. Neither of us looked back.

Though we struggled to understand each other, the only other person on earth who understood the depth and meaning of this moment was the man at my side. I knew Peter's feelings churned like mine, too overwhelming to express. We shared the end of our walk across America the same as the beginning, otherworldly and ordained, the church sermon ringing in my ears: "Will You Go with This Man?"

The adventures, dangers, hardships—the good and bad times—would surely forever cement us. I wasn't the best companion, wife, athlete, explorer, or lover, but nevertheless, every cell in my body shouted praise and glory. What a voyage it had been. My eyes were clear, the horizon was endless, and hope sprang with every proud moment.

The crowd was spread along the beach clapping and cheering as photographers and reporters followed us into the cold sea. We stood almost waist deep in waves that sent shivers up my legs and spine. The daring and charismatic man who had challenged a hillbilly girl from the Ozarks pulled me next to him as the ocean pushed and pulled us deeper into its own embrace. We hugged and kissed and raised our arms in victory. We had walked across America.

I noticed a small puffy cloud in the distance, just one in the unusually blue sky. Peter and I turned to walk back toward the beach. Sadly, I couldn't hold on to this milestone any more than I could hold on to that solitary cloud above us. Although the Pacific Ocean symbolized the culmination of our journey, the watershed moment was already slipping. It was here and now gone. A new world and life waited beyond this day because a baby was growing inside me. We had our next adventure, and I believed the days ahead would be full of happiness once we settled down and lived like normal people, no longer sleeping on the ground or walking fifteen to twenty miles per day. We were scheduled to write books, speak, and travel (by plane). We had opportunities like I had never known back in the Ozarks, and we had money. Yes sir, life would be a bowl of cherries!

I raised my arms toward heaven. Milo Franke's war cry whooped out of my mouth: "Glory to God!"

TWENTY-NINE

SLEEPING IN A BED

Slidell, Louisiana, Summer 1979

From coast to coast, newspapers and magazines published pictures and articles about our walk across America. One newspaper quoted Peter as saying, "There was no land left to walk. I was glad it was over, and I was sad." After the walk ended, we were whisked to the Mayflower Hotel, better known as the Grande Dame of Washington, DC. We lived in the luxury hotel for six weeks, compliments of *National Geographic*, while we wrote about walking three thousand miles from New Orleans to Oregon. The accommodations were extravagant, especially after years of sleeping on the ground. It felt strange because we had room service, and I could eat whatever and whenever I wanted. I slept on a pillow-top mattress with six-hundred-thread-count sheets. I was three months pregnant, and it was like sleeping on a cloud.

The hotel was a few blocks away from *National Geographic* headquarters, so we walked every day to the offices to sort through thousands of slides and review our journals from the road. No one hinted that we might be a cover story. Even the editors, Gilbert M. Grosvenor and Tom Smith, did not know our journey would become one of the most popular articles in the history of the magazine. Celebrityhood didn't happen because Peter and I were lucky, brave, or smart but because gifted senior editors like Tom Smith and Harvey Arden knew how to take our rough, raw material and make it shine. They were masters, and we learned a lot from them.

Seven months after we splashed into the Pacific Ocean, we were on the cover of the August 1979 issue of *National Geographic*. Subscribers around the world opened their mailboxes to see Peter and me with giant umbrellas attached to our backpacks hiking along a desolate road. We looked like a pair of intriguing, mind-bending humanoids from another planet. I was embarrassed of the picture. Vanity of vanities, I thought, *Did I really look like that?* I accepted it as another lesson in humility, but good Lord, did they have to pick *that* photo? It didn't really matter, because when the magazine arrived my belly was about to pop, and I wouldn't have cared if the magazine was a winning lottery ticket.

My pregnancy was not normal, and as Dr. Jack Andoni at Lakeside Hospital in Metairie prepared me for a cesarean section, I was terrified. The baby was positioned in transverse lie (horizontally across the uterus) with a dangling foot, so a natural birth was impossible. My uterus was heart-shaped instead of oval, and the baby couldn't turn or get into the birth canal. Plus, I had B negative blood *and* the RH factor. I thought my worries about crossing Oregon in the coldest winter since 1919 and being under deadlines at *National Geographic* were bad, and now this took the cake. I had to undergo surgery. I prayed nothing would be wrong with the baby. If the year had been 1879 instead of 1979, I would have died in childbirth, but our daughter was perfect. People from across America greeted Rebekah Pennell Jenkins, born on August 18, with hundreds of cards and letters.

Once the baby and I were released from the hospital, Peter drove us across Lake Pontchartrain to our first home in Slidell, Louisiana. It was a house with redwood siding and a gambrel roof on Doubloon Bayou. We'd agreed to return to Louisiana where we met and married, and we were excited for a place of our own, even though it was scary to have a mortgage. Our house sat near a dense swamp with cypress trees covered in Spanish moss, home to snakes and alligators. We lived just outside New Orleans and thirty minutes from the church where we were married and our best friends, Wally and Brenda Hebert, from seminary. I was so happy to have a healthy baby and thankful for a new house, but inwardly I was most thrilled to store my Jansport backpack in a closet.

The doctor told me not to lift anything heavier than the baby, to rest, and to make sure my incision didn't get infected. He said I could return to regular activities in eight weeks.

Are you kidding? I thought.

I had a baby to care for, a house to furnish, hundreds of thank-you letters to write, telephone calls to make, groceries to buy, and a book to help write. Two months was too long to be on the sidelines. Luckily, Mother and Dad came to help while I recovered from surgery. They were waiting at our house when we came home from the hospital, to greet us and hold their first grandchild.

The joy that comes with a new baby in the family is a celebration for everyone. Our family reunion lasted only three hours before Peter caught a flight to New York. He was scheduled to be on *Good Morning America* the next day and believed that national publicity was too important to pass up. Of course, I preferred him home with me and our newborn, but *GMA* was important. Peter was eager to tell the world about ending his walk across America, his next book, and our baby. I wanted to understand.

I kept trying to understand.

———————

Living together under one roof was not what I had imagined during the years we walked across America. Peter was unsettled. He paced the floor like a caged animal and couldn't sit still unless he was on the phone in his office. He loved talking on the phone; otherwise, he fidgeted, lost things, and tapped a pencil constantly on his desk. He forgot to pick up necessities at the grocery store like eggs, bread, or milk because his mind was somewhere else. When I asked for help with the baby or around the house, he seemed preoccupied. The most troubling thing was that he left home every night to drive around. I went to bed alone and never knew where he went or what he did. Often, I woke up after midnight when he came in. When I asked why he had to go somewhere *every night*, he said he couldn't be creative with a crying baby.

"Everything is on my shoulders!" he complained. "I have to figure out how to support this family and write my next book. I need space to be creative."

I wondered if his discontent came from being on the road for over five years and he needed more time to settle down. I questioned if he might be an adult with ADHD and racked my brain to figure out what was going on inside him. Instead of our lives settling into a comfortable rhythm on a quiet bayou, we moved faster than a speed boat.

Decorating the house, spending quiet evenings as a family, or cooking gourmet dishes fell by the wayside. If Rebekah and I didn't want to be alone, we would have to hit the road with Peter. I packed Halliburton suitcases and plenty of diapers, and off we went. I wanted us to be together as a family, and I understood that we had to make the most of our moment in the sun. We flew somewhere several times a month, and that appeased Peter, who accepted every speaking invitation or interview that came along. He insisted we had to strike while the iron was hot. Of course, he was right.

I bundled Rebekah, and we traveled to conferences, colleges, churches, meetings, and speaking engagements. Sometimes I appeared on television and radio programs with Peter, but most of the time, he appeared alone, which was fine with me. One week we were in New Mexico, the next week we were in Colorado, then Alabama and Mississippi. Weeks turned into months of being on the road, flying from city to city and staying in hotels.

When Rebekah was eight months old, we were in New York to meet with our book agent and William Morrow Publishers. We combined that trip with one to Connecticut so Peter's parents could meet their granddaughter for the first time. By then, Rebekah had been to half of the country.

Once we arrived in Greenwich, we slipped quietly through the front door on Pemberwick Road to surprise Peter's parents. They were upstairs painting the bedroom in their 1880s house. They didn't hear us come in. Just as Fred and Mary Jenkins started down the stairs, they saw Peter holding Rebekah, and they burst into tears. They squealed, laughed, hugged us, and sighed in amazement over their chubby granddaughter. I had never seen Peter's dad look more like a cuddly teddy bear.

"Oh, she looks so much like Peter!" Mary said. "It's like seeing him as a baby all over again."

Mary wiped a stream of tears from her cheek and said baby Rebekah was God's way of giving part of Peter back to them. It was an ecstatic reunion. I was proud to be the mother of their beautiful granddaughter and part of the Jenkins family legacy. Like we say in the South, I was tickled pink. It was more than I could have hoped for.

Our book, *A Walk Across America*, took off like a rocket. We sold more copies than we could keep up with. When the book was in its nineteenth hardcover printing, the pressure to write a bestselling sequel about our walk to Oregon was overwhelming. Before Peter left on another trip, he wrote a note to me: "Never have I been under more personal pressure. Sometimes I've wondered if I can handle it all, much less write a book that is as good or better than book #1."

It never occurred to me that my bold, daring, and charismatic husband might be afraid of failure. Now I understood why he was preoccupied and unsettled. We had moved from walking fifteen to twenty miles a day in nature to a jet-propelled, commercial world where he had no control. I told myself he needed encouragement and loving support instead of me nagging him to stay home with me and Rebekah.

Although he told me he loved me, I started to doubt it. Maybe he didn't want to be married or stay in one place. Maybe he simply couldn't settle down because he was a wayfarer at heart. I couldn't read his mind or solve the riddle.

Days before Rebekah's first birthday, Peter left for New York. I was sad because he missed her birthday and mine. If I ever complained, he would remind me, "What would it be like if we had to live like most people, punching a clock, worrying about making $200 a week with no future?"

Peter could never be a nine-to-five guy. And I didn't want him to be. He needed lots of space, and as a woman of faith, I needed to be patient. So I pushed aside my disappointment and kept my mouth shut, like I usually did, but I didn't like it.

Each time Peter came home, I felt hopeful. He was excited to see Rebekah and me and to settle down for a moment. But in less than a week he would be antsy again and planning another trip. He said he couldn't write a book with a noisy, rambunctious toddler in the house. Toddlers were even noisier than crying babies. His solution was to rent a cabin in Tennessee on Center Hill Lake, where there were no distractions.

Was I a distraction? I wondered.

He would be gone for months, and Rebekah and I would be alone. I was done being on the road, but he couldn't seem to stop.

THIRTY

THE TRAVELER

New Orleans, April 1975

Word spread on campus that the women in William Carey Hall were planning a dorm party to roast a couple of the professors. Free food and a room full of single women assured the gathering would be well attended, even though all the men ever did was blush and stare. Some of us thought a few professors were too straitlaced and needed a little laughter in their lives, so we prayed (though not very hard) that our roast would enliven the reserved academics and not offend them. After decades of reading, writing, and lecturing about church history, liturgy, the spread of Christianity, and more, the professors were universally stoic. In my opinion, they really did need to loosen up a bit.

The women's dorm lounge, crowded with students and professors and was loud when I arrived from my room on the second floor. Laughter erupted from all corners of the room. I wouldn't say the professors were loosened up, but they were smiling and occasionally laughing. It was certainly a start. I spotted my roommate, Ann, arranging some cheese and crackers and went over to help.

Looking out over the crowd from the small kitchenette, I noticed someone unfamiliar. I didn't recognize him as a student or professor, and by the looks of him, he didn't belong anywhere near a church or seminary. His wide forehead was framed by long, straight, reddish-blond hair, and his round, saucer-sized eyes were as clear as a glacier lake. He sported a scrappy beard on a face pink and taut from too much sun. His T-shirt clung tightly to his toned and muscular body, as though it needed to hang on for dear life, and his jeans and scuffed-up sneakers looked like they'd seen many more miles than they should have. He was strong, tall, and disarmingly handsome in a rugged sort of way—as if he might have jumped off a Gokstad ship from Scandinavia at the Port of New Orleans. The longer I stared, the more fascinated I became. He was exotic compared to the predictable, clean-cut seminary guys who lived in khakis and buttoned-up shirts. I wanted to know more and kept my ears open.

Later that night, I overheard a group of guys talking to the visitor and learned he was a Yankee from Connecticut walking across America for *National Geographic*. He had recently graduated from a small college in upstate New York with a degree in art and ceramics and wanted to see if America was worth saving after the traumas of the Vietnam War, Charles Manson, and Watergate. Disillusioned with a country that quaked in confusion, he told the men gathered around him that he liked the quiet environment on campus and thought it would be a good place to write. He liked that there weren't many distractions and planned to stay awhile. He didn't seem like the type who would be impressed by a hillbilly turned Yearbook Queen or campus socialite, but I hoped I would have an opportunity to meet him.

On a sticky spring night with the scent of jasmine in the air, a couple weeks after the roast, I was preparing food with other students in the women's dorm, and the smell of our fried hamburgers and potatoes brought a few friends through the door. We students didn't cook much, and the cafeteria served mostly bland corporate food. For many of us, these salt-and-grease aromas were the closest thing to home in the whole parish. Watching their mouths water but lamenting the fact that we hadn't bought extra hamburger patties, we invited our friends to join us.

While we ate and bantered, Don, a campus prankster and flirt, tossed a glass of water in a girl's face. She screamed like a cat and immediately threw a cup of water back in his face. Suddenly, water was spraying in all directions. It was a fully loaded water fight, and everyone in the kitchen joined in. Playful screams and whoops echoed through the entire building, and soon the kitchen and hallway were flooded like we had been hit by a Louisiana monsoon. For seminary students, it was as wild and carefree as Woodstock.

More students appeared to see what the hollering and laughing were all about, and it wasn't long before the water fight turned into a war, spilling out the front door. People grabbed anything that held water and indiscriminately started to douse each other. I didn't really know what had brought it out in us, but I was glad to see something shake up some excitement in the place. It was fun. Exhilarating. Rousing. I ran after one guy built like a string bean with a whole pail of water. As he saw me approaching, he raced toward the front door, threw it open, and narrowly escaped getting drenched. But there on the front steps stood the wide-eyed, red-bearded traveler who looked like a Viking.

I took one quick look at him and dumped the gallon of water over his head. The flicker in his bright blue eyes charmed me instantly.

He introduced himself as Peter Gorton Jenkins, and that's how I met my future husband.

THIRTY-ONE

WHERE KIDS AND CATTLE GROW

Middle Tennessee, 1982

A half-page story about Peter came out in the Sunday *Tennessean* while he was working on the manuscript at Center Hill Lake. In the photo, he wore jeans, a jacket, and cowboy boots and looked like the most chic author. The article detailed how he had isolated himself in a cabin for three months to write about walking from New Orleans to Oregon, while his wife remained at home in Louisiana with their daughter, who would be two in August. I didn't like being left alone but didn't think I had a choice. I started to grow accustomed to Peter's absence and stayed busy with Rebekah. I wrote my part of that book, *The Walk West*, when the baby was down for a nap or in bed for the night.

Peter was quoted in the paper as saying, "I fell in love with the South, which really surprised me because I was the typical snobbish Yankee. Most Southerners don't realize what they have; they don't realize the quality of life they enjoy."

He told the reporter he found Southern women to be the prettiest, the most feminine, and in a way, the strongest. The reporter wrote that Peter grinned when he said, "I did a real survey on my walk." I wished he had not said that because it stung and was embarrassing to me.

Days ran into months while Peter was in Tennessee. We each wrote our manuscripts in first person but didn't collaborate on the overall work, which symbolized the lack of communication between us. Our editor took the two manuscripts and fit them together. Surprisingly, it worked. *The Walk West* by Peter and Barbara Jenkins was published in November 1981 in time for Christmas sales. Publicity for the book was everywhere, from the *New York Times* to Christian bookstores.

"Join millions of others here and abroad, . . ." reviewers wrote. "Here's the book all America has been waiting for . . . the joyous, exultant journey that America took to its heart with love and pride."

The publisher was thrilled because presales were through the roof.

And the cycle began again. When Peter got home, the phone rang off the hook, and he was revved up day and night. He accepted every speaking invitation he could, reminding me that public speaking paid good money. When he left for Seattle to design promotional T-shirts, though, I was furious. He'd missed Rebekah's first birthday, and now he was going to miss her second. It felt intentional.

Something had to change because I was tired of pretending life after the walk was picture-perfect or that we had reached the Promised Land. Ernest Hemingway wrote, "The coward dies a thousand deaths . . . the brave, but one." I couldn't see it at the time, but Hemingway had me pegged. I was a coward.

I was afraid to confront Peter because it always ended in a painful and bludgeoning argument. He tried to convince me that I was too demanding, too religious, and everything he did was for his family. So I kept my mouth shut.

Fortunately, hope swept in when bravery wouldn't. Peter was so captivated by Tennessee that he wanted to move there. It didn't take much to convince me, because I wasn't crazy about living in the tropical heat and swamps of Slidell. I was inspired by the rolling hills, hardwood forests, green landscapes, clean air, waterfalls, country music, and turnip greens. The landscape reminded me of the Ozarks. It brought me closer to my roots. Both of us missed having four distinct seasons, and Tennessee offered all of them, but not too much of any.

Peter talked about the friendly, unpretentious people he believed would show him how to become a farmer and cattleman. I believed he wanted to live a simple country life and that we could all be happy. One reader wrote to us about the Volunteer State, "There is beauty in the open field, the woods and countryside, but most of all in the faces of my neighbors. I love them all. Spring Hill, Tennessee."

Tennessee sounded just about perfect to me.

Another attraction was our friends, Governor Lamar Alexander and his wife, Honey. Lamar had wanted an endorsement of his book titled: *Tennessean* and we immediately liked him because he walked over a thousand miles across the state to win the gubernatorial election in 1978. It was an easy and earnest friendship. Like us, fame was part of their lives, and before long, they were inviting us to parties and events at the governor's mansion. I felt welcome, and Peter was excited. Tennessee could be the safeguard our marriage needed.

When I was five months pregnant with our second child, we moved from the bayou to the picturesque and gentle hills of middle Tennessee. Native Tennesseans said a person could drop a seed anywhere in the ground and it would grow, so we accepted the challenge and bought a 135-acre farm south of Nashville. I fell in love with it.

The old house on the farm was built in the mid- to late-1800s. It had two tiny bedrooms, three fireplaces made with mud mortar, beaded ceilings and wainscoting, and floors of poplar—too small for a family of four, but we were enamored with it. We might build a new house eventually because our family was growing, but I hoped we could find a way to add on and make the little farmhouse work. It was as proud of its country heritage as I'd become of mine.

Our little farmhouse sat on a hill with a winding, clear creek across the front of the property. Deep springs provided water to the house, so we named our homestead Sweet Springs Farm. The barn, made of cedar logs, held stalls for horses as well as a large hay loft overhead. A smokehouse sat out back. All the buildings had hundred-year-old tin roofs. We were just a mile outside the tiny town of Spring Hill, Tennessee, population 1,100, and down the road from a Civil War mansion called Oaklawn. Our dear friend and Realtor, Martha Belle Smith, lived in the antebellum home where Confederate General John Bell Hood had slept the night before the Union army slipped by on its way to Franklin. Troops marched north of Martha's plantation and across our farm headed to the last battle of the Civil War on November 30, 1864. History of the war was buried on our land and for miles around. We found plenty of Minie ball bullets in our pastures.

On Sweet Springs Farm, I was the happiest I had ever been. This was my dream come true as we sat by a crackling wood stove, read stories to three-year-old Rebekah, and talked about our soon-to-arrive baby. The future was as bright as the fire in the stove, and I felt we were finally a family. My heart was happy for the first time since the walk ended. This move to Tennessee assured me the best days were ahead of us. Peter seemed happy too.

By December, we'd bought a tractor, a truck, and a trailer. Peter drove the pickup to a thick grove of trees on the back forty acres and chopped down an eleven-foot cedar tree. He brought the giant evergreen into the small farmhouse and anchored it in the corner of the living room. While I decorated, Peter threw more wood in the Buck stove to keep us warm. I was so full of joy I could burst. We were like a scene from Laura Ingalls Wilder's *Little House on the Prairie*. Little Rebekah helped me hang ornaments and strings of lights as we giggled and talked about baby Jesus.

———————

A few days before Christmas, my water broke, and I had to act quickly. Our second child was born by caesarean on December 19, and we brought him home on Christmas Eve wrapped in a big red stocking made by the Maury County Hospital Auxiliary. We laid Jedidiah Gorton Jenkins gently under the cedar tree for photos because he was our gift from heaven. His name meant "darling of the Lord." Peter was thrilled to have a son, and we spent our first Christmas as a happy little family around a wood stove and homegrown tree in a simple old farmhouse.

THIRTY-TWO

THE CALL OF THE ROAD

Spring Hill, Tennessee, 1983

W e loved the little old farmhouse so much we decided to save it and add on, restoring the original structure and adding 2,500 square feet of hand-hewn, red-oak posts and beams shipped from New England. I had no idea it would take eighteen months. While the renovation took place, we lived in a drafty house in town, but I went out to the farm every chance I could to see the re-creation of the farmhouse.

The construction team was led by Mr. Robert George from Columbia, Tennessee. This retired farmer and contractor displayed an aptitude for building things right the first time. We trusted him to turn our little nest into a classy farmhouse and a picturesque place to raise our children. Here, they would play in the creek, ride horses, fly kites, and learn the simple values of life.

Mr. George installed walnut floors and cherry paneling milled locally. He built a stacked stone hearth with a massive mantel of rocks from a nearby river. The original fireplace mantels and hand-carved front door were repaired and restored. William Morrow, our publisher, sent us museum paintings that featured scenes of farm life in the 1800s. Mr. George hung the murals in the dining room under a massive beam.

A New England craftsman built a masterpiece spiral staircase of mahogany and red oak that faced a stunning six-foot stained-glass window; the latter was made by a local glass artist and bordered with flowers from the states we'd walked across. The imposing cathedral ceiling in the kitchen showcased the hand-pegged beams, and every detail of the farmhouse captured natural materials and rural Tennessee history. It was perfect. I couldn't wait to move in.

Outside the house, the farm was growing too. We purchased three bulls and a bunch of cows with calves to start a herd. We had a big pond dug to water the livestock and bought a female husky named Lacey who had nine puppies. From there, we set up an office and hired an office manager and an associate to do research. We started a publishing company of our own called Sweet Springs Press at the same time the *Walk* books became the number-one and number-four bestselling paperbacks in the country. When we got word, I could hardly believe our books had been selected for the permanent White House Library. It felt like a dream to have such good fortune. Surely, it was meant for someone else. The windows of heaven opened even wider when a major Hollywood studio proposed making a movie. Life was such a whirlwind between writing and farming; I hired retired ladies to help with the kids, and they became like grandmothers to Rebekah and Jed. Even with the extra help, the mile-a-minute pace was a struggle for me.

One night there was a torrential downpour while we were still living in the drafty house in town that we planned to turn into offices. The house had high ceilings and four big rooms, so I made beds for the kids in the room closest to me. Peter was on another trip, so it was just the kids and me. Jed slept in a portable playpen, and I heard him whimper during the night. If he cried out, I'd crawl out of bed to check on him, but unless he wailed, I was simply too exhausted to get up. He whimpered softly and fell back to sleep. It was ecstasy to hear the steady drum of rain on the roof and drift back to sleep.

The next morning, I went straight to Jed's bed and my jaw dropped open. My baby boy was huddled in the far corner of his crib, and his hair, body, and crib were soaking wet. It was a mystery until I looked overhead and saw a hole in the roof over the playpen. Jed had been rained on all night. I couldn't believe my baby had slept in the rain, and I was thankful he didn't get sick. I was tired of the pressures of our busy life, and I didn't want to raise our children alone. I couldn't. It was clear that something needed to change.

Jed was fifteen months old when we learned he needed surgery to correct inguinal hernias. I sat on the window ledge in his room in Vanderbilt Children's Hospital with my knees under my chin, fighting tears as I waited for doctors to come get him. He lay strapped to the bed with tubes coming out of his arms and nose. I had spent most of the night worrying and saying prayers as I watched the dreary February rain turn to snow. Outside, people scurried in every direction. They looked busy and rushed, caught up in the pace of life, and I wondered how many had ever sat all night at the bedside of a sick child. Again, I was alone because Peter was traveling.

Before I could wipe the smeared mascara off my face, I heard a knock on the door. It was Reverend Homer Kelly, our small-town pastor, the one who shouted the gospel on Sundays and cried when people gave their hearts to the Lord.

He said, "If there's anybody here that needs me, anytime, day or night, I'll crawl to get to you, if need be!"

I knew it had been no easy task for him to drive from Spring Hill to Vanderbilt, over thirty miles, because he could only see out of one eye and hear out of one ear. Like the Good Shepherd, Pastor Kelly always went to see about one of his flock. He prayed for baby Jed, for me, and for Peter. I appreciated him but longed to have my husband by my side. Unfortunately, Tennessee had not been the answer I'd hoped it would be. Instead of a close-knit family with two parents sharing life together, I was all but a single parent with the responsibility of raising our children alone, as well as overseeing the farm, office, and business affairs.

Whenever he was in town, Peter returned to his old habit of being gone until midnight or later. I didn't know where he went or what he did. He said he needed quiet time to think about Jenkins & Associates, Inc. We were a bona fide corporation with employees, deadlines, and a pile of projects. He was always busy with a deal, promoting a book, or preparing to speak somewhere. I was sad and lonely, but he was under more pressure than ever, and I convinced myself that I needed to let him be. The closeness we had enjoyed our first Christmas in Tennessee was long gone. We passed each other in the kitchen and on the way out the door. We were business partners who happened to be authors who happened to be married with kids. I wrote in my journal, "When Peter and I are alone, there is nothing personal to talk about, only books and business. Romance has wilted. I am dead."

Since Peter wasn't ever home when I went to bed, physical intimacy was nearly nonexistent, and it came as a complete shock when I found out I was pregnant again. I called the office of my ob-gyn for the test results. I felt worried and full of questions when the nurse delivered the news. I was definitely pregnant.

Would a third baby turn things around?

Bring us together?

Be yet another new beginning?

I tried to think positively, but it didn't last long.

Something was seriously wrong. Peter was colder, more distant, and critical of me. I speculated, prayed, and jumped through hoops to avoid arguments and make him happy. I was codependent and a people pleaser before I knew what those terms meant. He ignored me unless he had an audience. Then he'd call me honey and his Southern belle. By this point, I knew he didn't mean it. My insides were in knots.

During my third pregnancy, I was pale, weak, and sick as a dog. Most of all, I was tired. I didn't know a woman could be alive and feel so weary and lifeless. I had no energy to chase baby Jed or supervise Rebekah's efforts at modeling clay. I couldn't hold down a saltine cracker and was stunned speechless when Peter announced he was leaving to climb Mount Everest. He waited weeks before he steered the conversation toward China and said, "By the way, what do you think about me going?" He claimed he had always wanted to go, but this was the first I had heard of it.

After eight years of marriage and walking across America with Peter, I knew he was a nomad, but *this*?

He said he wouldn't go if I felt *super* strongly about it. Well, damn, I *did* feel super strongly, but I was too much of a coward to say anything. If I opposed him going, he would claim I was keeping him from gathering material for another bestseller. He took my silence as agreement. One reporter quoted him saying, "Barbara wanted me to go. She told me to go."

That simply wasn't true. I was dutiful and compliant, and I kept my mouth shut. If I opposed him, he twisted my words until I appeared selfish, a drag, or too uptight.

"All you do is feel sorry for yourself," he would say. "Why don't you move back to the Ozarks with the rest of the losers in your family?"

Flashes of my hillbilly childhood would return to me, and I'd think, *He's right. I'm unworthy. I'm as stupid and silly as a goose!*

Although my self-confidence was below ground level, I still couldn't understand how any husband and father would intentionally leave his near-term pregnant wife and two young children.

He argued he had to stay on the road to support us and the affluent lifestyle I wanted. This felt like an arrow in my heart because what I wanted was for him to be a husband and father.

———

I laid my bloated body on the sofa and told myself to stop letting him browbeat me. I had to learn to stand up and quit allowing myself to be exploited. I had to set boundaries. Somehow, someday I was determined to hold my own. At that moment, however, I didn't have the energy to beg, "Please, don't go."

When Peter and his new research assistant, a recent divorcée and single mother of two children who lived in Michigan, planned to leave for China, I was in my eighth month of pregnancy. Jed was in diapers, and Rebekah had turned five.

John Steinbeck wrote in *Travels with Charley*, "We do not take a trip; a trip takes us. The honest bookkeeper, the faithful wife, the earnest scholar gets little of our attention compared to the embezzler, the tramp, the cheat." John Steinbeck was a prophet.

Peter was enthralled with his new adventure, and nothing could stop him. The call of the road pulled him, but I was beginning to wonder if something else did too.

THIRTY-THREE

REVIVAL

New Orleans, 1975

Peter Gorton Jenkins was a great romantic, a storybook hero, the man of my dreams. It wasn't long after our soaked introduction that our relationship blossomed into a stormy, runaway romance. He was dynamic, fun, and daring. I admired his bold and fearless approach to life. I wasn't sure exactly what I was searching for, but somehow he embodied it. He showered me with attention and affection, far more than I had ever experienced in my life. Some evenings he would stand under my dorm window and throw pebbles until I appeared. When I opened the window and looked down, he would be standing there like a wild, restless Romeo with stars in his eyes, wildflowers in his hands, heart on his sleeve.

Nobody had ever been that wild about me or openly demonstrative with their feelings toward me. My former fiancé from my college days had loved me deeply but quietly. The boys in high school may have admired me, but the notes they left in my yearbook were cordial and passionless. When I was a little girl on the wrong side of the tracks, I *never* heard the words, "I love you," and I can only remember a few embraces—from Granny. To Peter, I was manna from heaven. Whatever it was he was out looking for across America, he had found some of it in me, though I couldn't begin to explain what that might have been.

Peter was the first Yankee I had ever known. I learned about his New England roots, and he learned about my Ozark hillbilly upbringing. It didn't take long before he nicknamed me Country Girl. We took long walks across the seventy-five-acre seminary campus in New Orleans and talked about everything imaginable. We talked about the North and South, politics, poverty, wealth, art, music, race, drugs, communes, religion, money, and more. Our discussions were lively, and we would banter until we were exhausted. Then we'd hop into the VW and head for the French Quarter to find a jazz band to dance to and drink beer. Before the night was over, we'd wind down with chicory coffee and powdery beignets at Café du Monde. I spent all my free time with him and yearned for each night to last longer. Our relationship moved quickly from flirting to deep late-night talks to passionate good-night kisses.

He wasn't perfect. I learned Peter had a colorful history of girlfriends and lovers, and I worried his former relationships and party-boy ways were a red flag. He even attended the *real* Woodstock and made no secret of the many blurry nights and hazy mornings in his past. It made me nervous; seminary was a far cry from a free love and drug festival, but I reasoned Peter's womanizing ways were over and gone. Just before we met, he had turned his life over to Christ at a James Robison Crusade, an old-fashioned Southern revival. He was born again, and that meant he was a new creature in Jesus Christ. Forgiveness was the core of the gospel, so if Peter's wild ways were forgiven, who was I to hold them against him? Besides, how could I cast the first stone, when I had sown plenty of wild oats myself?

Whenever I doubted him, he'd prove himself with the right smile, the right kiss, or a handwritten invitation.

To Miss Barbara Jo Pennell, Carey Hall, to partake with Mr. Peter Jenkins a moonlight picnic at the lake and a dance of delight somewhere in nightly New Orleans. Please reply by 7:00 this evening.

I always replied yes.

THIRTY-FOUR

PIECES OF THE PUZZLE

Spring Hill, Tennessee, 1984

My time to deliver our third child was near. I drove to Walmart to pick up dog food, and when I tried to pick up a bag, I almost fainted. I managed to get a clerk to bring a chair for me to sit in. She asked if there was anything she could do or someone she could call.

"Sure, if you want to call China," I said.

A look of worry crossed her face, and when I saw how concerned she was for me, I started to cry. I felt foolish and out of control as I struggled to compose myself. The girl thought I was upset because I couldn't lift a bag of dog food, but I was crying for a thousand unspoken reasons.

As I waddled out the door, my tennis shoes were untied and I almost tripped. I tried to bend over to fix them but couldn't. A woman passing by saw my predicament and kindly tied them for me while I fought back more tears. No one in the store recognized me as the woman who had walked across America, and there wasn't any danger of it because I could hardly make the trip across the parking lot. All they saw was a pregnant woman who needed help.

Shortly before I entered Maury County Regional Hospital, Peter returned to the United States. My caesarean was real trouble this time. The epidural didn't take, and they had to give me a spinal block. My uterus was as thin as Saran wrap, and when my blood pressure fell dangerously low, the surgical team jumped into action and tilted the operating table straight up so my feet were above my head.

A good friend of mine was a registered nurse and stayed in the operating room with me. She held my hand and stroked my forehead as my teeth chattered. She tried to explain what was happening without scaring me to death. I had never heard of a doctor using forceps during a caesarean, but my ob-gyn nearly pulled me off the table trying to get the baby out. He was wedged on one side of my deformed uterus, and there was no other way to grab him.

A normal C-section took forty-five minutes from start to finish, but I was on the operating table for three hours. It was worth it when I laid eyes on my son, round and pink with a deep dimple in the middle of his chin. I wasn't aware of the risks or possible neurological injury to the baby after such a difficult delivery. All I could do was sigh with relief. Soon, I faded into a blissful sleep.

Luke Lavell Jenkins was born and joined the 1 percent of the world's population with red hair and blue eyes. I chuckled recalling that Mark Twain wrote, "While the rest of the planet is descended from apes, redheads are descended from cats."

Luke was definitely the son of Peter Jenkins and looked just like him. Redheads symbolized magnetism, produced their own vitamin

D, and needed fewer painkillers to treat ailments. I was thankful Luke's infant body could handle pain because he would require several surgeries when he was older. He was born with a deformed foot, hemangioma, and panhypopituitarism—an underdeveloped pituitary gland. He would need to take a growth hormone to help him develop properly.

On the way home from the hospital, the atmosphere was frosty between me and Peter. I didn't want to hear about his trip to Mount Everest or anything else he had done. I wasn't charmed by him. I needed a long recovery and a partner.

What lifted my spirits was moving out of the rickety, drafty house in town and back into the "new" farmhouse. I had spent over a year living in disorder and out of boxes. Our clothes had been hung on nails on the back of doors, and hot and cold air had whistled through floors between which you could see the ground.

Rebekah and Jed were rambunctious as we moved boxes to the farmhouse. I packed clothes while I watched baby Luke in his bassinet. Jed and Rebekah played chase until I heard blood-curdling screams. Jed pulled Rebekah's hair, and she screamed for me to punish him.

"Stop it!" I said. "Jed, don't you pull anyone's hair, or you're in big trouble!" I shook my finger and meant business.

Jed looked back and forth, and his eyes twinkled. The wheels turned in his toddler brain until they landed on his best answer: "Can I pull my hair?"

With Peter gone most of the time, it was the children who brought laughter, joy, and adventure to my life. And they could find it nearly anywhere.

———————

That winter we settled into the farmhouse, I was thrilled. Everything in the kitchen and bathrooms worked, and we were finally warm. Peter left on another trip to Michigan and then to Vermont to become a spokesperson for a New England shoe and boot company. I was consumed with keeping the fires burning at home, taking care of the children, and writing *The Road Unseen*. I didn't have time to monitor where Peter was going or what he was doing. He said his secretary had his schedule if I wanted to know where to reach him.

On a cold blue night on the farm at minus seventeen degrees, Rebekah and I stayed close to the wood stove, letting the fire warm us as we watched the winter sky. The moon hung just outside the kitchen window. It looked like a broken fingernail, a silver crescent in the middle of blinking stars above. I could hear the crackle of the logs and would throw more on the fire as soon as I finished bedtime stories with Rebekah. The little boys were already asleep. Peter called, as he did every night, and ended the conversation with "I love you," but his words were empty and distant and felt as cold as the weather outside. Raising three children, writing, and living every day with a heavy heart because of the state of my marriage was too much. I decided it was time to sort things out.

———————

One week when Peter was home, I kept a diary of his routine. Monday: left home at 8:00 p.m.; Tuesday: gone overnight. Wednesday: gone to a dinner meeting. Thursday: gone and returned after midnight. Friday: gone and returned 2:00 a.m. This was his modus operandi.

I finally asked him to consider going to a marriage counselor with me. He agreed, but we'd gone to only two appointments when he told me *I* was the one who needed a counselor.

The fissures in our marriage spread like cracks in a windshield, and pieces to the puzzle unexpectedly began to appear. Out of nowhere, and unsolicited, anonymous phone calls started coming from Texas, Missouri, California, Michigan, and other parts of the country, and I couldn't believe what people told me. They were mistaken. Outright lies. Peter was preoccupied, verbally abusive, and inconsiderate, sure, but would never do the things these people said he'd done! He said he loved me. He said he loved me *just last night*.

One day, a caller left a message on our home answering machine: "I just saw Peter Jenkins on Christian television. How long is he going to get away with what he's doing? Isn't there someone who can stop him? It's a mockery to Christianity!"

The nation Peter had romanced was not as blind as I was.

The office staff knew things were off-kilter as well, but they tried to be discreet. No one wanted to hurt me. I didn't understand why Peter's associate suddenly quit to take another job. It would be a long time before I learned that he'd refused to cover for Peter any longer. The secretary didn't want to say anything because I was on the cover of *Today's Christian Woman*, working on a manuscript, and juggling children. We had a thriving business with more opportunities in one year than most people had in a lifetime. We were a symbol of faith and family. But at what cost?

One time I awakened during the wee hours of the morning and heard Peter downstairs in the library on the phone. I tiptoed to the balcony and overheard him in hushed and alluring whispers. His laughter was low and sensual. My heart pounded as I remembered the anonymous phone calls and now this. The revelation shook me to the core while our innocent children slept in their rooms. To keep the peace and not rock the boat, I had chosen to be blind. I could no longer deny the obvious. The truth made me physically sick as I quietly crawled back into bed and screamed on the inside, *Why, dear God?*

Why would Peter betray me and his children?

I didn't know how to feel, but a resolve from deep within began to surface, like a smoldering ember. It must have been buried in my Ozark soul, an inheritance from my fiery mother. Whatever it was, a switch flipped. I had to get my rear end in gear. The kingdom was about to come crashing down.

THIRTY-FIVE

HEADED TO ANOTHER CIVIL WAR

Spring Hill, Tennessee, 1986

I knew Peter would fight 'til death do us part, but the door to my heart had slammed shut and I was done. I collected records of calls to Michigan that were dated long before I became pregnant with Luke. There were ten calls a day, some three hours long and late at night. Many other calls took place in the mornings from a pay phone where Peter dropped Rebekah off at school. In those days, the home phone bills were itemized so the data didn't lie.

I dug up credit card and hotel receipts and knew the identities of two women and possibly three more. With the anonymous calls from several states, I wondered how many women were out there. I could barely function as I looked into the fair, freckled faces of my children and knew their idyllic world was coming to an end. When I walked across America, I had lived through all kinds of danger, but I feared what lay ahead would be far worse. I wasn't sure I could survive.

The last straw came a couple weeks before Christmas 1986. Peter was on a monthlong publicity tour for *Across China*, so I had time to gather documents after the office was closed for the day. One evening while I was there, one of our teenage babysitters saw the car and stopped in. She'd assumed Peter was working late. Her father had passed away, so Peter had stepped up as a loving male figure. I knew she would be upset when I told her what I was doing and why, but I wasn't going to lie. I spoke slowly and tenderly as I broke the news that my husband was unfaithful.

The blood drained from her face, and she turned ashen.

"Oh, Barbara, I never meant to hurt you," she said, tears spilling down her cheeks.

"What? What are you talking about?" I asked.

She started to sob and choked on her words. She'd recently turned eighteen and lost her virginity to my husband.

The air went out of me like a punctured tire.

For the next few moments, I was nothing but an empty shell. Robotically, I asked questions.

Even in my stupor, I had enough wherewithal to realize the babysitter was just a kid mesmerized by a famous man who paid attention to her. No doubt, she believed she was in love. I couldn't absorb one more betrayal.

I filed for divorce the next day, and the babysitter agreed to testify for me in a deposition.

"Barbara Jenkins Seeks Divorce" read the headlines.

News of our breakup traveled faster than a shotgun blast. Readers from New York to Los Angeles wanted to know details.

They wanted dirt. They wanted gossip. I had to change my telephone number, keep the front gate to the farm locked, and hide out while I tried to protect the children and make it one day to the next. I was heartbroken, embarrassed, ashamed, and scared for our safety. I wanted to crawl into a hole and never come out. All that I stood for as a Christian had been a farce. I had been living a lie.

Peter continued his book tour and gave interviews, trying to put rumors to rest. While he was gone, I quietly and methodically closed the office; shut down Jenkins & Associates, bank accounts, and credit cards; let the staff go, packed Peter's clothes and mementos; and left his car parked at the airport full of his belongings. He knew a volcano had erupted and was desperate to stop the damage. He asked famous Christians to talk sense into me. At the same time, *Across China* jumped onto the *New York Times* bestseller list.

News of our divorce was bad publicity for the book, and Peter hired a prominent Nashville attorney to send a press release across America: "Writer Peter Jenkins hopes for reconciliation with his wife who has asked him for a divorce after 11 years of marriage. Peter loves her very much and is hoping that things work out."

When fans read the news, saw it on TV, or heard it on the radio, jaws dropped and people were stunned. Everyone wanted to save the sweetheart couple and wondered why on earth I would file for divorce when my husband was publicly proclaiming his love. He wanted to save the marriage. Cards and letters came asking me not to destroy our beautiful testimony. One person said I should not feed my baser instincts of selfishness and pride. Famous ministers and Christian authors called and without asking what had happened pleaded with me to reconcile because thousands, perhaps millions, of lost souls had come to know the Lord through us. "Love covers a multitude of sins," they wrote to me.

They scolded, begged, and preached about God hating divorce and implied I should fix whatever the problems were. Each letter made my heart hemorrhage with fresh blood, as if I were being slaughtered over and over.

I was thirty-nine years old and physically healthy, but the pressure was crushing, and I lost sleep and dropped twenty pounds. I pondered the remains of my life as I took long drives through the countryside hoping to find peace and direction. I was an Ozarks hillbilly who had achieved more than I ever imagined, but as quickly as fame and fortune had appeared, they were going down the drain. I had to sort through the trauma and prepare for the upcoming trial, but first, I was going to be deposed.

I sat at a long conference table in a fancy office in downtown Nashville with four lawyers, two legal aides, and a court reporter. Across from me were Peter's three high-powered attorneys and their intrusive questions. Peter was not in the room, thank God. I never imagined ending up here and worried about crumbling under examination or blubbering like a silly goose. They didn't know how afraid I was, but I told myself I had to hold it together. I stared across the table. These litigators were more threatening than any outlaws I'd met on the road.

My deposition would be used by Peter's legal team in the upcoming trial. I was told to expect several hours of questioning. The court reporter stretched her fingers and started to type. The clicking keys were piercing in the hushed room. Every word had to be recorded because Peter was countersuing me for custody of the children, child support from me, and more than half our assets.

One of the first questions stunned me.

"Mrs. Jenkins, have you ever sought counseling in regard to your drinking?"

I laughed out loud. Except for an occasional glass of wine at dinner, with friends, or at a social event, I was practically a teetotaler. Besides, I'd been pregnant for the better part of five years.

Otherwise, the line of inquiry jumped from my past work and educational experience, business, and friends to what I planned to do in the future. After the first hour or two, the lawyers moved toward more private and intimate details.

Had we sought marriage counseling?

Had I sought counseling for myself?

Had I ever been romantically involved with someone else?

Did I have any romantic interests at this point?

Then, Peter's high-profile attorney looked me squarely in the face and asked, "Now, Mrs. Jenkins, can you honestly say you had nothing to do with the downfall of your marriage?"

"Well, sir," I took a deep breath. "Yes, I did have a part in the downfall of my marriage."

The attorney had a half grin on his face. He titled his head and fixed his eyes on me, assured my answer would incriminate me. He waited like a fox for me to trip up and say something he could use in the trial.

In a soft voice laced with iron, I went on, "Yes, sir, I contributed to the downfall of my marriage because I should have kicked Peter Jenkins in the ass a long time ago!" Mother would have been proud.

The Chancery Court was on the second floor of the Courthouse in Maury County. The walls were cold, and the floors looked like mirrors. Everything about this building reflected Tennessee life: births, deaths, marriages, murders, divorces, and property taxes. I knew I would become another statistic as I walked into the courtroom where legal gladiators were primed to fight. Reporters sat in the back and waited. They'd been told that the testimony could be sordid and long.

Peter and his high-powered team sat at a long table that faced the judge's bench, while I sat at a table with my one attorney on the other side. I didn't look at Peter because I was afraid I might cry. Peter's legal army planned to prove that the ideas for our bestsellers and the writing of the books were his work alone. Therefore, they would argue that Peter was entitled to most of our assets and 100 percent of the rights to *A Walk Across America* and *Across China*. On the floor beside Peter and his lawyers were boxes of documents that verified assets, publishing ventures, books, royalties, and rights.

It worried me to be outnumbered, and I realized I could lose. I could walk out of here today sharing custody of our children and nothing else. My attorney had a few scribbled notes. Everything else was in his head. He stood up to address the room.

"May it please the Court, I'm a member of the Nashville Bar, and I represent Mrs. Jenkins in this proceeding," he said. "Mr. and Mrs. Jenkins will have soon been married twelve years and have three small children who live with their mother and have since the separation."

He walked around the table like a slow bear and stopped before the judge. He said, "Mr. Jenkins takes the position that *A Walk Across America* is his separate property, but we believe the proof will show that it was written while Mr. and Mrs. Jenkins were walking across the western half of the US and during the winter they spent in Colorado. Mr. Jenkins is asking for joint custody of their three children, and we believe that the proof will be that Mrs. Jenkins has taken care of the children since birth by reason of his travels and work habits."

Every word was deliberate, unyielding, and straightforward.

"Now, in addition to asking for full custody of the children, Mrs. Jenkins asks the court to award her an equal share of all the assets," my attorney concluded.

Peter's attorney jumped to his feet in response. "The evidence will show that Peter Jenkins began contemplating the idea to walk across the United States long before he met Barbara Jenkins. We submit that when this trial is over, there will be no question in anyone's mind that Peter Jenkins created almost all the marital estate which Mrs. Jenkins now selfishly attempts to take away from him."

He continued talking about how Peter came from humble beginnings and that I had more potential for employment because of my education. Hearing this made my blood simmer, but my attorney advised me to stay calm and not show emotion. I had to appear collected at all times.

And these were just the opening statements.

Once the trial started, I was first to take the stand. Peter's attorney circled in front of the judge and then turned to me, asking, "Will you agree with me, ma'am, that you have never received any formal education or training in regard to being an author and in regard to writing?"

How odd, I thought. *Why would he ask those kinds of questions? Wasn't this a trial about adultery and inhumane treatment?*

I knew nothing about litigation strategy or that his goal was to protect Peter's assets from me. My attorney told me not to be scared and to simply tell the truth.

"I studied journalism in college and we received training from *National Geographic* magazine, our book publisher, and editors. I was right there by Peter's side. We learned together," I answered.

"Mrs. Jenkins, it was Peter Jenkins who caused you to become interested in the possibilities of writing books, isn't that the truth of the matter? Don't you give Peter Jenkins, this relationship, any credit for your becoming interested in pursuing the writing profession?"

Again, I didn't understand where he was going with this questioning.

I said, "I give Peter Jenkins and the opportunities that came our way a lot of credit. They all developed my interest in writing, not just Peter's. If I weren't interested or motivated inwardly, another person couldn't make me interested in anything."

"Ma'am, those books caused you to become an established and recognized author in your own right, do you agree with that?" the lawyer spat. "And you became a celebrity due to those books and the ensuing publicity, didn't you?"

I paused a moment before I answered. "I think I was a sleeping celebrity—someone behind the scenes because I was not accessible. I was at home having babies."

As the day wore on, several unexplainable recesses occurred where Peter's attorneys and my one attorney left the courtroom and huddled with the judge in his quarters. It was a legal chess game in which every player had to make the right move. However, it was played, the futures of my children were at stake, and I was terrified. Before the day ended, something unexpected happened.

The lawyers and the judge walked back into the courtroom after a long recess. My attorney approached me with a stoic face and said, "They withdrew the countersuit."

He never told me why, and to this day, I don't know why Peter withdrew.

The next day, a *Nashville Banner* headline read, "Divorce Trial Gets Touch of Mystery." The article said, "The divorce trial of nationally known authors Peter and Barbara Jenkins took on an element of mystery Tuesday when the judge in the case accepted a sealed deposition."

The reporters didn't know what to make of it.

Another headline read, "Jenkins Withdraws Countersuit, Peter Jenkins Admitted Fault in his Divorce Trial."

Until the third and last day of the trial, the attorneys haggled over why I dissolved our jointly owned corporation, and finally, the judge asked the lawyers if they wanted him to grant the divorce. All of them stood quickly to their feet, "Yes, your Honor, we are in agreement on that point."

There was no hesitation, and the judge said, "All right."

It was over.

I had walked three thousand miles on foot, coauthored a shelf of bestsellers, helped build a sizable estate, and given birth to three children. And with two words from the judge—"All right"—the curtains closed. The end.

There would never be another "Barbara and Peter."

I swallowed hard and looked away as I gathered my things from the flat table where I had sat for the past three days. My heels clicked across the tile floor as I headed out of the building to my car like a dead woman walking. Damn this moment! Damn this day!

I drove home in a daze and pulled the station wagon up to the beautiful farmhouse and stopped. Drained and lifeless, I was glad the kids were with relatives and I didn't have to face them. I was a mess and needed to cry, scream, throw things, fall on my knees, and finally, pass out from exhaustion. I dropped my purse and keys on the kitchen counter and saw a printed note from my daughter: "You're the best. We love you. You can do anything. We hope you had a great day. I love you. From Beka, Jed, and Luke."

It broke me. I sobbed until I ran out of tears.

THIRTY-SIX

AN INVITATION

New Orleans, 1975

Peter lived in the men's dorm while he worked on his first article for *National Geographic*. One afternoon he handed me twenty-five pages and asked if I'd like to read what he'd been working on. I was impressed with his storytelling and thought his writing was captivating. However, his manuscript needed a good edit to make it shine even brighter.

I finally asked if he would like help with his draft, and he accepted, but when I started to cross out words, correct grammar, and move paragraphs, he resisted. Every mark I made turned into a heated debate. He didn't like how freely I severed sentences and rearranged blocks of text. I could tell it made him nervous but also that he knew he needed the help. What he was doing was important. I believed in his mission and in him and wanted to help make his manuscript even more compelling.

Peter was dynamic, fun, and daring. I admired his bold and fearless approach to life, and he certainly embodied the excitement

I craved. We spent every day together for eight months. One day Peter came to me and announced that he had to get back on the road. The article we had worked on together was finally finished and submitted to *National Geographic*. New Orleans was just the halfway point of his journey. He had thousands of miles left to go, and it was time to head west.

I felt sad when he told me his plans because I had strong feelings for him and didn't want him to leave. I guess he felt the same way because he began to pressure me to come with him.

"Barbara, why don't you join me?" he asked.

"You're kidding, right?" I scoffed.

I couldn't comprehend such a monumental feat by anyone, much less by me. I was shocked, but he was serious.

Our relationship had become something far more than I expected, but walking across America was Peter's dream, not mine. I had my own future. I had another year to finish my master's program. I wanted to find a good-paying job and make a good life for myself. At least, I thought I did. That flicker for something more was always burning inside me. That spark led me from the Ozarks to New Orleans to Peter, and it was still burning. I still had a childlike curiosity, a sense of wonder, and dreams of things I wanted to do.

I told him I would think about it.

Even though I was starting to imagine spending my life with Peter, I was convinced what he really needed was a tough outdoors woman, not me. I was too feminine, too prissy, too frightened, and too insecure, but Peter held a bulldog belief that I was meant to join him on the rest of his journey. I had never met a man with dreams bigger than mine. I was confused and didn't know what to do. Our feelings for each other were certainly mutual, but I didn't have the desire, physical strength, or skills needed to undertake such a long physical endeavor.

Our budding relationship was at a crossroads, and I knew that whatever I decided was going to hurt both of us.

CHAPTER THIRTY-SEVEN

DON'T WORRY, BE HAPPY

Spring Hill, Tennessee, 1988

The hit song in 1988 was "Don't Worry, Be Happy" by Bobby McFerrin, and it became my mantra. I was determined to pick up the pieces and move on with my life. It was going to take time to untangle my mind, heal my heart, and straighten out the complications of both my finances and my feelings after the divorce. I was content and carefree one minute, and worried and in tears the next. My children were young, impressionable, and full of energy, but the weight of single parenting overwhelmed me. Because Peter had been gone 95 percent of the time, I had plenty of experience being on my own, but I didn't know how I was going to raise three children on a few hundred dollars a month of child support.

Court dockets were full of penniless felons and broke defendants, so an author with property and assets did not win much sympathy from the judge. In addition, my attorney charged

$50,000 in legal fees, and there's no telling what Peter's team of lawyers charged him.

Fortunately, I was awarded half the rights to our books, the restored farmhouse, and thirty-seven acres of land. Peter was awarded the remainder of our farm. Good or bad, owning property meant I had paper assets, but I needed actual dollars to pay bills, buy gas, and get groceries. The book royalties weren't going to cover much, and my farmhouse and land couldn't be sold overnight unless I wanted to give them away. I had to figure something out. I was raised on nothing. I could do it again.

I never lost the ability to pinch pennies, and while some children begged for expensive toys, my kids preferred to play with sticks and stones in the creek and chase rabbits in the fields. As months and years passed, my share of book residuals diminished even further, so I clipped coupons, shopped at thrift stores, and browsed flea markets. I finally rented out the farmhouse, and between rental income, child support, and dwindling royalties, I paid the bills, kept a roof over our heads, and put food on the table and gas in the car. I wanted to write more books, even write a novel, but discovered book publishers viewed me differently from Peter. He was the writer, front-runner, celebrity, and pied piper, and I was merely the ex-wife. Peter continued to make book deals with large advances. It was another gut punch, but I would pick up the pieces and keep going. That was what hillbillies did.

In spring 1989, a year after the divorce was final and a year of putting my nose to the grindstone, the kids and I needed a change of scenery, so I packed the station wagon, and we left early one morning on a road trip. I asked Martha Smith, who lived in the Civil War antebellum mansion down the road and had sold the farm to Peter and me years earlier, to join me and the kids on a road trip out West. She was recently retired, and we'd become close friends. She was my confidante, mother figure, friend, and one heck of a smart businesswoman. She taught me about real estate and investing, assuring me that better days lay ahead. The children loved her and called her Dandy. They were thrilled when I told them she would be coming along on the adventure. Luke was still too little for such a long journey, so I left him with Dot Murphy, one of the older nannies who adored him, and he was treated like the little prince he was.

After a few days, we found ourselves headed west on an isolated road in New Mexico, the same one Peter and I had walked many years earlier. Suddenly, I spotted a herd of antelope and pointed them out to Rebekah and Jed, who squealed with wonder just as I had the first time I locked eyes with the glorious creatures. They were exactly as I remembered them: doe-eyed, elegant, and curious, but I was a different woman from the one who had walked through these prairies all those years ago.

I carried heavy sorrows because of my failed marriage, but the walk was not one of them. I delighted in pointing out windmills to the children where their dad and I had drank water, or bridges under which we had slept.

"Why did you sleep under there?" Rebekah asked, her nine-year-old eyes wide and shining.

I explained how important it was to camp in a safe spot and how I used a dry cow patty for a pillow under that bridge.

"What's a cow patty?" Jed asked.

Martha cut her eyes over at me and chuckled. How was I going to explain dried cow dung to Jed?

"You don't know what a cow patty is, carrot face?" Rebekah said.

"I'm not a carrot face!" Jed countered with a strong punch.

Rebekah screamed, Jed hollered, and a full-blown fight erupted in the back of the station wagon. Fists flew before I pulled over on an incline to stop the nonsense.

"Hey! Look up there!" I yelled above the wrestling match. "Look! Look!"

Rebekah and Jed froze in place. I pointed straight ahead at what looked like a row of layered ice cream cones on the horizon: the magnificent Rocky Mountains. The golden glow of the setting sun was behind them.

Jed stared thoughtfully at the snow-capped peaks and asked, "Who lets down the snow? God or Santa Claus?"

Seeing just one leg of the walk through my children's eyes made every blistered step and every lawsuit that followed worthwhile.

We enjoyed trout fishing, hiking trails, renting a jeep, and spotting elk in the high country of Colorado, and then we drove back east to the rolling countryside, soft breezes, and starry nights of Tennessee. Our road-weary hearts were full, but little did we know, our slice of paradise on Sweet Springs Farm would soon turn into a prison cell.

Ten months after our divorce was final, Peter took Rebekah, Jed, and Luke to Michigan. It was his weekend for visitation, and unknown to me, he was getting married to his research assistant in Michigan. The kids never said a word about being in a formal church wedding and probably didn't know it was happening until they got there. I was shocked. Even more shocking was when Peter brought his new bride and her children to live in the ranch house across the field one week later. Peter and his new family were going to be our neighbors.

As soon as the newlyweds moved next door and across the field, they strolled hand in hand in view of my kitchen window. They laughed and talked playfully and walked leisurely through the tall grass like carefree teenagers. Peter appeared, for once, not to be in a rush. He wasn't yelling at her to hurry or stop whining. It was salt in my wounds. Even though he had been with other women while we were married, I wasn't ready to see it.

Every time the kids played in the backyard, Peter called them to come over to his house or took them for rides on his tractor. The kids were confused by the complicated family dynamics with their father and new stepfamily next door and didn't know how to express their thoughts and feelings. They certainly didn't understand what had happened. Peter was gone, and then he was everywhere with a new wife and other children.

The new Mrs. Jenkins enrolled her children in the same schools as mine, parked in my space at the bus stop, and joined the same local organizations to which I belonged. My children were told to call her Mom, and it was a fresh twist of the knife every time they talked about her. There were no boundaries. Even Peter's cattle broke the fence, destroying my garden, grass, shrubs, and boxwoods, eating from all the fruit trees up and down the driveway and leaving mountains of manure.

Six months of blurred boundaries was all I could take. Martha found a place for me to rent, so I closed the farmhouse with everything in it, packed up the kids and our Welsh corgi, Cocoa, and moved into a tiny furnished house in Nashville to start a new life. Night after night when I said prayers with Rebekah, Jed, and Luke they cried for their dad to come back and asked why we had to move away.

"Do we have to call her Mom?" they asked.

I told myself not to worry because we were going to make it, and come hell or high water I was going to be happy! We were barely unpacked before Peter filed a motion asking the judge to stop my move to a different county.

I laughed out loud. We were just thirty minutes away, and I was done being told by Peter Jenkins what I was thinking and feeling and what I could and could not do. It wasn't his adventure anymore; it was mine.

THIRTY-EIGHT

PUT THAT IN YOUR PIPE AND SMOKE IT!

Nashville, 1991

Nashville was exactly what I needed. It was a town where no one knew or cared about my story, and it was easier for the kids too. Although I missed living in the country, urban life embraced us. I enrolled the kids in school, and they made friends quickly. Doors opened for me to meet other parents and attend school functions. We started a new life, and my children led the way.

Martha was on the lookout and found an older home for us to buy: a 1960s four-bedroom with a big yard on a dead-end street surrounded by hundreds of acres of virgin forest. I used my farmhouse as collateral and bought it for a pittance. Rebekah and the boys had plenty of room to ride bikes, climb trees, and explore the woods. It was like we were back in the country. Herds of deer, flocks of wild turkey, rabbits, squirrels, fox, hoot owls, and occasional raccoons and possums passed through regularly. There were no antelope, but wherever they were, I could feel them smiling on us.

Before the kids were old enough to drive, I spent every day hauling them from place to place: three different schools, the pediatric endocrinology clinic at Vanderbilt, soccer practice, piano, and dance. We attended Woodmont Baptist Church whenever the doors were open. On school nights, I helped with homework, washed clothes, cooked, cleaned, and went to bed exhausted. I still worried about bills and Peter's next lawsuit (there would be more to come), but somehow, we were making it work. There weren't enough hours in the day for me to consider holding down an outside job, so I did my best with what I had. When I needed help, I learned to ask for it.

I called foundations for assistance with Luke's medications, haggled with the health insurance company, and staved off collection agencies with payments of twenty-five dollars a month. Luke's growth hormone was $8,000 a month, and my insurance paid only a portion. When the medical bills mounted to $50,000, my only option was to file a lawsuit to force Peter to contribute. The divorce decree did not require him to assist with medical or educational expenses. I hated to do it and wanted to be able to handle things on my own. "You're a loser and should go back to the Ozarks" rang in my ears.

Even when I felt like a washed-up divorced woman with three kids and a drained bank account, not everyone saw me that way.

Honey Alexander, the governor's wife, and a compassionate friend invited me to be part of the Tennessee Women's Forum, a chapter of the International Women's Forum, made up of over 4,000 top women leaders around the world. The women in Tennessee were statewide (even national) influencers, such as supreme court judges, lawyers, CEOs of large corporations, bank presidents, and more. New members had to be invited to join, and I was surprised she thought of me, but I agreed to join. I guess I had some notoriety as a coauthor of bestsellers, but in my mind, I was unimportant and didn't deserve to be a member. I felt uncomfortable because I was among the most influential women in the state. In the beginning, I kept quiet at meetings. I didn't want to speak out of turn or embarrass myself, but eventually, I started opening up. Shortly after I became a member, Luke's school asked me to sit on their board, and before long, I was asked to be chairman. One invitation led to another until two governors of Tennessee (one Republican and one Democrat) invited me to serve on commissions. I figured it was because people thought I had nothing better to do with my time since I didn't have a "real" job. To my surprise, the day came when I was voted president of the Tennessee Women's Forum. It was years before I realized they saw something in me that I didn't always see in myself, a flicker I'd carried with me all my life, a smoldering ember from back in the hills of the Ozarks.

———————

The kids called my parents MeMe and PaPa. They still lived in the Ozarks and had a barn, pond, and fruit orchard surrounded by a grove of woods. The kids loved to visit them. Dad tinkered with tools in his barn and took the boys to fish in the pond, while Mother made homemade donuts and cookies and baked anything they wanted in her old Home Comfort wood cookstove. They made crafts, painted pictures, and worked in the garden by day. They played board games and cards by the woodstove at night.

Mother oozed affection for Rebekah, Jed, and Luke, which tempered the memories of criticism and harshness toward me when I was growing up. We never spoke of it, but I believe the pain and resentment I harbored toward Mother was healed by my children. Maybe reconciliation comes to every family when a new generation arrives. All that mattered was that Mother's old heart had softened and so had mine.

I'll never forget leaving them the day after Christmas 1989, our bellies still full of roast turkey, sweet potatoes, mashed potatoes and gravy, deviled eggs, home-canned green beans, fruit and cranberry salad, homemade bread, and fresh pumpkin pie. I looked back at Mother and Daddy. They stood in their gravel driveway beside their small house looking longingly and blinking back tears. They waved goodbye until we were out of sight.

On the long eight-hour drive back to Nashville, I savored our Christmas with MeMe and PaPa and thought about my hillbilly parents and grandparents. I was beginning to see them differently than I ever had. Mother and Daddy were growing old, softer, more open and demonstrative with their feelings. I saw their kindness, honesty, work ethic, and needs, even though they never claimed to have any. How could they not melt every time Rebekah, Jed, or Luke threw their arms around their old necks and told them they were the best MeMe and PaPa in the whole wide world? My children were the lights in their lives. Their old hearts were full when the kids squealed over Christmas presents, humble gifts as they were. Mother and Daddy lived on a meager Social Security check and couldn't afford much, so they saved all year to buy toys at Walmart, flea markets, or yard sales for Christmas.

They wanted to know when we were coming back. When would they see us again? Mother and Daddy were keenly aware of the fleeting time and knew the importance of being together before it was too late.

I was deep in thought about my Ozarks roots when the station wagon gave a jerk and started to rock and sway. The kids screamed as I brought the car to a bumpy stop on the side of I-24. My tire had blown out.

A wave of loneliness and winter drizzle washed over me when I got out of the car. I had never changed a tire, but it was time to learn. I wiped rain out of my eyes and struggled to figure out how the jack worked as I knelt at the rear bumper. Cars whizzed by. The kids were getting impatient. I cut my finger, and it began to bleed badly.

A pickup truck pulled up behind me. It sat there with windshield wipers slapping and headlights shining on me as I knelt on the ground tugging with the jack. My kids' faces were pressed to the fogged windows. I knew they were scared; I'm sure I was scared too. After the divorce I had a hard time trusting people.

Finally, two men emerged from the truck. I looked up through soggy hair and saw one of them wore a cowboy hat and the other a farm cap. They looked to be in their midtwenties.

"Need some help, ma'am?" asked the one in a cowboy hat. His voice was kind and respectful. From the looks and sounds of them, they were good country boys.

"Ma'am, you get back in the car and we'll fix this," one said.

In only a few minutes they'd replaced the blown-out tire with the temporary spare that looked like a donut. It was good for thirty miles, and I had 100 to go. When I told the young men I was headed to Nashville, they shook their heads and said I'd never make it.

"Is there somewhere I can buy a tire?" I asked.

"Closest place is toward Eddyville, up in Kentucky," they guessed.

After a few minutes trying to give me directions, they smiled and said they would lead the way. It was twenty miles of back roads in Kentucky.

The young men honked, and pointed out the window at the filling station, and drove away. Thank God Almighty it was open the day after Christmas.

Inside the station hung calendars of half-naked women, and there were two grease-covered older men who looked like they chewed nails for breakfast. The deep creases in their faces looked like tractor ruts; cigarettes hung out of the corners of their mouths, and one had a beer belly. This wasn't the local Quick Stop.

When I told the men my predicament, they studied the blown-out tire without expression, puffed their cigarettes, and mumbled to each other.

"Umm, we may have one tire that'll fit'er," said the man with the beer belly.

They grunted, cussed, smoked, and worked for almost two hours before they finally got the tire off the rim. I was worried this was going to cost an arm and a leg. I wasn't sure they'd ever seen a credit card, and I didn't have enough cash to pay for a new tire and two hours of labor. This whole thing might be $150 to $200.

Meanwhile, the kids stayed in the station wagon and played with their Christmas toys. At least, that's what I thought they were doing.

Instead, the boys had found a box of my sanitary napkins and pulled every single one apart. It looked like a white cotton field from one end of the station wagon to the other. The old mechanics stared at the boys and the remains of my maxi pads but never uttered a word.

Finally, one man wiped his hand on an oily towel and said, "We got 'er fixed."

Here it comes, I thought.

"That'll be three dollars for the used tire and four dollars labor," he said with one eye closed from a trail of cigarette smoke. "Yep, that'll be seven dollars in all." He seemed proud of himself for adding it up.

"What?" I shrieked. "That can't be right. I owe you a lot more than that!" I stammered about how I could pay them much more with my credit card if they would take it. I continued to blubber.

"It's Christmas!" said the greasy mechanic with the beer belly.

"But, but . . . you worked so long and hard to fix it," I gushed.

"It's Christmas," he said with finality. He looked away because he wasn't going to argue or accept more than seven dollars. The two men grunted and mumbled to each other in mechanic talk. Our conversation was over.

They pointed me back to the interstate, and I drove home realizing that not every stranger was a murderer or cheat. A Scripture verse came to mind: "Be not forgetful to entertain strangers: for thereby some have entertained angels unawares" (Hebrews 13:2 KJV).

The longer I was divorced, the more I learned to accept help from others. One of my greatest supports was a group of ladies called 12 Women, patterned after the twelve disciples. We met in my home weekly for two years and then monthly for many more years. We had a different leader and topic each week, followed by heartfelt discussions. The diversity among us brought balance and perspective to our discussions, and as our friendships deepened, all of us became better and stronger people. I wrote a guidebook for 12 Women groups to start around the country, and they did.

Each woman in our original 12 Women was a trailblazer in her own right:

- Patsy (deceased): event company owner and cowriter of hit songs
- Carolyn: poet, artist, and designer
- Charlotte: pastor's wife and seminar leader
- Susan (deceased): television producer and writer
- Pamela: contractor and music event company owner
- Jan: community and church volunteer
- Betty: medical and electrical sales
- Pam: television advertising and sales
- Judy: hit recording artist and vocal coach
- Diane: Emmy-nominated television writer and producer
- Elaine: owner of production and communications company
- Barbara Jo: I didn't have a job or a title, so I wasn't sure what I was.

Over time, I learned that regardless of impressive resumes and public images, everyone in 12 Women experienced problems, victories, and defeats. They had insecurities and needed understanding and support just like me. I wasn't alone. Accepting help from these women emboldened me to keep going. I was tired of struggling, haggling with collectors, and clipping coupons. Old voices that whispered I wasn't worth anything faded. I was beginning to feel more confident and no longer saw myself as someone walking a half mile behind my husband, just trying to keep up. One day, I scraped together enough courage to contact one of the largest corporations in the world.

The Hospital Corporation of America had purchased ninety acres from Peter and paid him millions for the very land he and I had purchased when we bought the farm. But he was awarded those acres in our divorce. I resented his good fortune and yelled at God about how unfair it was. I was still clipping coupons and struggling to pay the bills. I wanted to know, however, what HCA planned to do with the property because it was adjacent to mine. I felt foolish calling a Fortune 500 company to request a meeting with the VP of real estate development, but somehow, I got a meeting.

With sweaty palms and my heart in my throat, I walked into the HCA building with a blueprint of my property. My acreage ran along Saturn Parkway with an exit that dropped off in front of my land. My property was the crème de la crème. If Peter's was worth something, mine was worth something too.

"I'm here today as your neighbor," I said to the middle-aged man dressed in a starched shirt and horn-rimmed glasses. We made small talk about the weather and traffic until I sensed it was the right time to ask him what HCA planned to do with the property they'd bought from Peter. He told me their long-range plans, which were big and wonderful. They would start with an emergency center and expand from there.

"As you know, our properties join. My parents are elderly and in declining health, so I need to focus on them," I announced.

He looked puzzled and wondered where I was going with the conversation.

"I wanted you to be the first to know that I'm considering selling some of my acreage." The executive froze in place and turned a milky white. For a moment, I thought he was having a stroke or something.

He caught his breath and blurted, "You're not going to sell to Maury County Regional Hospital, are you?"

He looked terrified at the thought. HCA was embroiled in a five-year, multi-million dollar lawsuit with Maury County Regional Hospital, which wanted to block HCA from building a hospital on the land they had purchased from Peter.

"No, sir," I said. "No one knows about this, not even my grown children. I wanted you to be the first to know and give you the opportunity to make an offer."

I paused to make sure the man was still conscious. I told him I didn't have a lawyer or a real estate agent, and if HCA was interested, the deal would be between HCA and me. No one else. I told him I didn't want publicity or the city of Spring Hill to know anything about it.

His face was flushed as he explained HCA didn't need more land and they were years away from building a medical campus because of the lawsuit. Of course, I understood his position and explained I was just being a good neighbor. He ran his fingers through his hair and nervously asked me to not do anything until he talked to his people.

I thanked him for seeing me and left his office. I walked out of the building knowing HCA was over a barrel. They didn't need my property, but HCA could not allow someone else to buy it, especially Maury Regional.

Months later, I sold thirty-two acres to HCA. I was able to keep my beautiful farmhouse and five acres. The deal allowed me to pay off the mortgage on the farmhouse, pay off the mortgage on my house in Nashville, and pay off old medical bills. For the first time in my adult life, I was debt free. There was enough money left over to set up a rental property business with tax-deferred exchanges and avoid capital gains. It all boiled down to this: I would never have to clip coupons again.

All I could think of is what the ol' timers in the Ozarks used to say: "Put that in your pipe and smoke it!"

THIRTY-NINE

OLD WOMAN IN
A WHEELCHAIR

New Orleans, November 1975

I t was a clear, crisp fall day when we rode in my car to the Word of Faith Temple located near Lake Pontchartrain. Peter parked the car, and we got out without saying a word. We were talked out and argued out, and I was prayed out. After two weeks of thinking and praying over his proposition, I agreed to go to church with him one more time. I wanted to end the pain and tell Peter we should part ways. I wasn't going to walk across the country with him. I simply wasn't capable.

Sundays at the nondenominational church were different from the Baptist services I had attended all my life. Word of Faith Temple had a full orchestra, celebrity-bound singers, and a variety of preachers, and each time somebody stood at the pulpit was unpredictable, unscripted, and powerful. The sermons went far beyond three points and an altar call. It was riveting. The minister was Reverend Charles Green, a middle-aged man from Mississippi. Although short in stature, Brother Green projected the aura of a prophet. He was a 1970s protégé of Moses leading his people out of bondage and into the Promised Land. He preached with fire and passion, much more so than pastors at other churches I attended.

We arrived late. Thousands of people were seated in the auditorium when the usher motioned for us to follow him down the aisle, through the crowd, and to the only two open seats in the front row.

The last place I wanted to sit was in the front row. We usually sat in the back so no one could see the holes in Peter's shoes and jeans.

As we walked toward the front of the building, I felt embarrassed. Too many eyes were watching us make our way to our seats, located a few feet from the podium. We were so close, I could see every wrinkle on Brother Green's face. The lights dimmed. I took a long, deep, sorrowful breath. I knew this was my last day with Peter.

We sank into comfortable, theater-like seats, and Brother Green announced a special guest preacher was visiting from Detroit, Michigan. At least today's sermon would be a distraction from the anxiety and tension I felt. With every second, I felt pieces of Peter and of myself slipping away. Brother Green asked the congregation to give a big welcome to eighty-one-year-old Mom Beall, a small woman who sat to the left of the pulpit in a wheelchair. I was startled because in the Ozarks, women were not allowed to preach.

Mom Beall was introduced as the founder of the largest church in Detroit. We were told that she was recognized as the mother of the Latter Rain Movement, an outpouring of the Holy Spirit. It seemed like a lot of woo-woo mumbo jumbo to me, but I didn't really care. These were my last hours with Peter. I had waited faithfully for my miracle, and time had all but run out. I didn't think there was much that an old woman in a wheelchair could do to change things. She didn't look like she was about to turn water into wine. Born in 1894, Mom Beall had no formal religious training. She wasn't unlike some of the women I'd grown up with in the Ozarks, an old worn-out soul, nothing more than a glorified religious housewife and mother. I was studying to earn a real religious diploma, and at that moment, I felt somewhat superior.

Brother Green pushed Mom Beall to the front and handed her a microphone. Her voice was soft, and her smile was sweet. Her old eyes panned the crowd like we were a sea of grandchildren, wide-eyed and ready for story time. She directed everyone to chapter 24 in the Book of Genesis. A swoosh of pages crossed the auditorium; these were the days when people brought Bibles to church.

We turned to the story of Abraham and Sarah, a simple old couple. In the story, God promised them a baby, and Sarah laughed at the very idea because she was far beyond childbearing age. To their amazement, Sarah got pregnant and gave birth to a child when she was *ninety* years old. They named their baby boy Isaac, which means "one who laughs."

When Isaac grew up, Abraham wanted his son to marry a girl from his homeland, so he sent a servant to find a wife for his son. Abraham made the servant take an oath to find a wife for Isaac, but if the woman was unwilling, the servant was released from his vow. Mom Beall leaned into the microphone and cooed like a mourning dove as she recounted a story we had all heard a hundred times before but were suddenly captivated by. She told us the servant found a beautiful young woman at a well and knew she was the one for Isaac. The girl's name was Rebekah. Her family became excited over the proposal, but they wanted Rebekah to make her own decision. Her family said, "Let's call the young woman and ask her about it."

So they called Rebekah and asked her.

Mom Beall smiled sweetly and said, "The title of my sermon today is. . . ."

Her voice trailed to a whisper. You could have heard a feather drop. Thousands of people sat motionless. Suddenly, Mom Beall broke into a thunderous voice and halted after each word. She drew out her words, long and slow, as she said, "The title of my sermon is . . . 'Will . . . You . . . Go . . . with . . . This . . . Man?'"

Her words hummed across the auditorium like volts of electricity. I felt like I'd been struck.

Did she just say that?

The words pierced me, and I held my breath, afraid to look over at Peter. I felt as if a heavenly finger were pointing directly at me. It was as if *I* were the young woman being asked to go to foreign lands, leave everything behind, and walk into an unknown future. *This* was my sign. I just knew it from the top of my head to the tips of my toes.

Mom Beall kept the congregation spellbound for forty-five minutes. She told us that Rebekah agreed to go with the man, and then she shouted, "It's wonderful when God gets rid of stuff. It's worth everything to be free! I don't want you traveling with the pack. God calls each of us separately."

Like Moses coming down from the mountain, Mom Beall had holy fire all over her body and her words. I was wide-eyed and speechless and had fallen off my high horse.

When the last song from the choir was sung and the last prayer spoken, the church service ended, and the crowd filed through the exit doors. Families laughed and people chatted about where to eat lunch. I was reeling on the inside. I was weak, exhausted, and convinced my knees would buckle when I stood up.

The odds of me hearing this sermon on the very day I was going to break up with Peter was mind-blowing. The timing of "Will You Go with This Man?" packed a life-changing punch. Like Rebekah in the story and sermon, I was being given a choice to go with Peter or not. This was the sign I had been praying for. This was Moses parting the Red Sea. This was my calling from God.

I shook as I reached for Peter's hand and leaned on his strong arm. My whisper was barely audible, but I knew Peter heard me say I would go. God already knew.

FORTY

THE WORLD IS
YOUR OYSTER

America, Africa, Europe,
South America, 2005

Dozens of men and wild-eyed women are all asked the same question: "Can you find love again?" It was too complicated with my first marriage, very over the children, and the one serious relationship I had ended fast. Once the ink was dry on the HCA deal, my floodgates opened, and the world became my oyster. I was finally free to go. I fell in love with the world, the places I traveled, and what each new day promised.

———

Before Rebekah left for college, we flew to Zimbabwe on a mission trip. After Joberg's 1980s prop planes, we flew over the African plains, where elephants and giraffes traveled together looking like small figurines. We floated down the Zambezi River with hippos in

THE WORLD IS
YOUR OYSTER

America, Africa, Europe,
South America, 2000s

D ivorced and widowed women are all asked the same question: Did you find love again? It was too complicated with my three growing, very creative children, and the one serious relationship I had didn't last. Once the ink was dry on the HCA deal, the floodgates opened, and the world became my oyster. I was free and ready to go. I fell in love with the world, the places I traveled, and what each new day promised.

———

Before Rebekah left for college, we flew to Zimbabwe on a mission trip. After boarding a 1940s prop plane, we flew over the African plains, where elephants and giraffes traveled together looking like small figurines. We floated down the Zambezi River with hippos in the water and monkeys swinging from the trees. We visited Victoria Falls, one of the most spectacular wonders of the world. We helped with young children at a remote mission near Harare and slept in a bunk house under netting to fend off mosquitos, spiders, and poisonous snakes.

When we returned, I bought a small motor home and learned how to drive it. It handled like a pickup truck and was easy to park and hook up in campgrounds. I named it *The Mother Ship* and soon hit the road with Betty and Pam, my single friends from church. We took off to the Telluride Film Festival, California wine country, the San Juan Islands, British Columbia, Niagara Falls, New York, New England, all the way down to the Gulf of Mexico, and through the Everglades. On one trip, we outran a tornado in Kansas. Another time, we ran out of gas in the middle of nowhere beside the California State Penitentiary.

Another friend, Jennifer, walked with me through the ruins of Ephesus, Turkey, where we stood in colosseums where gladiators had fought and sang hymns in a cave called St. Peter's, right near the Syrian border, where the first Christians had worshipped. We toured the iconic Hagia Sophia, sailed on the Bosphorus Sea, had Turkish baths, and got lost in Istanbul. Later, we hopped islands in Hawaii walking black-sand beaches, eating fresh guava, and standing underneath the oldest tree on Maui, which covered an entire city block. On Michigan's Mackinac Island we walked, rode bikes, or flagged down horse-drawn taxis because no cars were allowed. Jennifer was always ready to go somewhere and had toured the world as a long-time backup singer for Dolly Parton.

Luke, his beautiful wife, Anna, and I traveled to Quito, Ecuador, the second highest city in the world at 9,352 feet above sea level. We stood on the equator, existing for a moment in both the Northern and Southern Hemispheres. In a tiny car the size of a roller skate, we drove on desolate roads, passing Quechua shepherds herding sheep in the Andes, and got lost in the jungle.

There was Nova Scotia with Elaine, where we ate lobster, toured historic towns, and saw candy-striped lighthouses. There was the Alps with Glenda, where I rode the rails in Switzerland, drank beer in Austria, and walked around Lake Como in Italy. There was Engineer Pass again, standing in the Rockies at 13,000 feet. This time, I traveled by jeep through steep canyons and harrowing switchbacks. Then there was South America with Jed.

After he worked five years for a peacekeeping organization called Invisible Children, Jed left on a quest of self-discovery and planned to write a book, just as Peter and I had. For eighteen months and 10,000 miles, he bicycled from Oregon to Patagonia in southern Chile. He and a buddy started in Oregon where Peter and I had finished our walk across America. Friends joined him on occasion, but some of the time, Jed traveled alone. After my journey, I couldn't tell him not to go, so I asked every person I knew to pray for his safety. Every time my phone pinged with a message from Jed, I thanked God. I worried daily about everything from cartel violence to venomous snakes. It was a tremendous relief the day he reached the end of his journey at Punta Arenas, the southern tip of South America.

When I stepped off the plane, Jed was there to meet me, and he looked strong, healthy, and fit.

"Hola, Mamacita!" he cheered as we hugged each other. I was glad he spoke Spanish because all I could do was use sign language, grin a lot, and look totally lost.

His friends, Sophia Bush, an actress, and Bridget Connelly, founder of Luna Bay Kombucha, would join us at the airport within the hour. The four of us planned to celebrate the end of Jed's bike trip and his thirty-second birthday. Then we would explore glaciers, hike mountains, and eat at the best restaurants.

It was December 2014 and summer in South America. The days were long, and it didn't get dark until 11:00 p.m., so all we needed were light jackets and snacks for a short day hike in the Torres del Paine National Park. We rented an SUV and drove a couple hours north of our Airbnb to the park on an empty two-lane road with wild guanacos that looked like llamas, grazing on the shoulder. Off in the distance we saw the famous granite peaks of Torres del Paine towering 8,200 feet above sea level. The jagged, snow-capped peaks pierced a perfect blue sky that played host to a rare and breathtaking condor.

We were confident we had plenty of time for a short six-mile hike into the park to a hidden glacier lake at the base of the granite peaks. At the park gate house and lodge, we met a handful of other hikers from around the world who assured us that the hike was definitely worth it. I was excited, and after years of adventuring, I felt bulletproof. I didn't notice that the hikers were all young enough to be my children—my grandchildren, even.

We strapped on our day packs and began the journey up, up, and up. I had hiked across the Rockies, but this was the most rugged landscape my feet had ever trekked. There were boulders the size of dumpsters, loose rocks, dangerous drop-offs, swinging bridges over rushing glacier rivers, thick forests with exposed roots, and bitterly cold winds that threatened to blow us off the trail. We didn't know the park was famous for its strong gusts or that we were here during the windiest season. It was clear straightaway that I was no longer the twentysomething girl who had walked across America. I was sixty something, with a bad knee.

About halfway up, I told Jed, Sophia, and Bridget to go on ahead. I would follow (slowly) behind. They quickly bounded out of sight like baby rabbits while I plodded along and crawled over one boulder at a time. At the higher elevation, the skies were cloudy and gray, and a cold misty rain started. The higher I climbed, the less oxygen there was. It was grueling, my lungs stung like they were frostbitten, and I wondered if I would make it to see the famous view. Every step was a test of pride as young hikers started to descend and passed me like smiling roadrunners. They looked at me with compassion, I thought, or maybe it was pity.

I looked up and saw Jed and the girls coming down. They were radiant and said it was the most spectacular view anywhere on planet earth. They had snapped pictures of each other in the twilight and in front of the secret turquoise lake with the towering sword-like granite peaks in the background. I was only two hundred feet from reaching the top, but the wind howled and rain started to pour.

Jed and the girls were surprised to see me because they thought I had turned back long ago, but they cheered me on, reminding me how courageous I was. I really wanted to reach the top, but the rain turned to sleet. I figured if Moses never made it to the Promised Land after all he had been through, I shouldn't be embarrassed to turn around and head down. I had seen plenty, and I knew Jed and the girls had taken lots of pictures.

I thought the climb up was severe, but going down made my feet and legs scream. I was certain I would need knee replacement, maybe the hips, too, by the time I reached the bottom. I worried about what would happen if I tripped on a rock and broke an ankle. There were no park rangers or rescue squads in this part of Patagonia, and no cell phone service. It was 10:00 p.m., and darkness would be upon us in one hour. We faced another five hazardous miles back to the lodge.

Jed told Sophia and Bridget to hurry ahead, and he would stay with me. I was glad for two walking sticks to steady my steps because every minute we lost light. The wind blew at hurricane force as the sky turned darker. There was no moonlight and no stars over this part of South America. It was the blackest night I had ever experienced in my life.

Jed was out in front, but it was the blind leading the blind. We felt our way over boulders, crept across swinging bridges, slid down vertical rocks, and shivered in the wind. Inch by inch we made our way. Out of nowhere came a torrential downpour, and a flurry of icy needles stabbed my face. I was exhausted through and through, soaking wet, and cold to the bone. In some moments I didn't believe I was going to make it. It crossed my mind that I might die out here at the end of the world. I started to pray and remembered the children's book *The Little Engine That Could*, repeating to myself over and over, "I think I can, I think I can!"

It was 1:00 a.m. and within a mile of the lodge when, suddenly, I couldn't hear Jed—only whistling wind and pouring rain. Water pounded against my face in the pitch black as I yelled for him, but I heard no answer. I hollered louder. No answer. A sense of terror I'd never known swept through me as I wondered where he was.

Did he fall off the trail?

What happened to him?

Why won't he answer?

My voice was high and shrill when I yelled Jed's name a third time.

The flashlight on his phone blinked on. He pointed the beam in my eyes and said, "You got a problem, Mom?"

I screamed, "You little smart aleck!"

I could have killed him on the spot but was too relieved to know my son was all right—and that he hadn't lost his sense of humor.

Just then, we saw a tiny flicker of light off in the distance through the freezing rain.

"I think I can, I think I can," I said to myself as I dragged my weary body another mile down the black trail in pounding sleet.

Numb and ready to drop, I hobbled to the entrance of the lodge and wondered if I had hypothermia. I was so tired and cold I didn't have the energy to shiver. Inside, Sophia and Bridget asked the staff to keep the front doors open until we got there. The girls found something to eat and had hot tea and toddies waiting for us. It was pushing 2:00 a.m. when I stumbled in and collapsed on a chair. It took a few minutes before I could sip the hot toddy, and when I did, it went down slowly and warmed my insides. My body started to thaw. I was too exhausted to speak and wasn't sure this ol' hillbilly gal from the Ozarks would ever go on another adventure.

I took another sip of hot whisky and felt the fire and heat move through me. My blood warmed, and a spark of life came back. I closed my eyes and thought again, "Naw . . . tomorrow's another day."

EPILOGUE

All I carried forth carries on further.

Rebekah found her niche as a Belmont University scholar with a master's degree in creative writing. She became a book editor and had her own imprint at a publishing company. Later, she taught English literature at two colleges and continues to work with a nonprofit coaching ministry. Her latest passion is horses. She and her champion quarter horse Scooter compete in western riding across the mid-South. She's a real life cowgirl. Rebekah and her husband, Jonathan, are the doting parents of Josephine.

Jed was student body president at Franklin Road Academy and graduated from the University of Southern California and, later, from Pepperdine Law School. Jed has written *New York Times* bestsellers and just finished his third book. Would you believe it's about me and our political, social, and generational differences and how we maintain a loving relationship? He lives in Los Angeles but travels around the globe gathering fodder for his next books. He loves nature and outdoor adventure and leads writers' conferences all over the country. His sense of wonder and quick wit are the life of every party.

Luke was awarded Outstanding Leader at Benton Hall Academy and attended Western Kentucky University. He worked for Hilton Hotels and handled property management for several years. Today, he is the owner of a real estate business, and he loves to golf, fish, camp, and compete in gaming. By the way, the growth hormone worked, because Luke is almost six feet tall. He married beautiful Anna, and they are the loving parents of Lyla Estelle.

Each of my children worked through growing up in a broken home, but those are their stories to tell.

After my granddaughter Josephine turned nine, she read *I Once Knew a Woman*, a collection of profiles I wrote many years ago about the women I met on my walk across America.

"Yo Yo, that book was the *b-e-s-t* book I've ever read!" she said.

She was excited, and her eyes widened. I chuckled because she had not read many books, but her approval meant everything to me.

My granddaughters link me to my granny from the Ozarks who never had more than a cotton dress and tattered apron but still somehow had deep and unwavering love to give.

Once, when Lyla just was five years old, she sat quietly behind me in her car seat as we were on our way to get ice cream.

"Yo Yo, I love you!" she said out of the blue and as a matter of fact.

I looked at her in the rearview mirror and smiled.

"Well, sweetheart, I love you to the moon and back."

"No-o-o, Yo Yo!" she scolded. "I don't mean like that! I mean, I love you in my spirit!"

Those generational chords of love—past, present, and future—are the ties that bind and hold us on course through the ages. There is a reason we need to listen to those who have gone before us. It is our greatest inheritance.

Did I regret growing up in the Ozarks as a poor hillbilly? Goodness, no! My upbringing taught me hard work, grit, humility, to appreciate simple things, and not to get a "big head." My parents and grandparents were the salt of the earth. Abe Lincoln said it best: "God must love the common man because He made so many of them."

When I look back, I think most of my mother's harshness and criticism came from her own fears and insecurities and weren't about me. Although I never understood her mercurial behavior, I loved her with my whole heart and believe she did the best she could. I found a letter she instructed to be read after she was gone. *"When I am gone and you feel forlorn, look up above, you won't be alone. At Heaven's gate, I'll wait for you with arms outstretched and Grannie, too. Just know my love is always near."* I give Betty Jo (aka MeMe) credit for giving me her enormous gift of creativity, a fire in my belly, and a determination to amount to something.

Did I regret marrying Peter Jenkins? Honestly, no. He will forever be the starry-eyed young man who threw pebbles at my dorm window and captured my heart and imagination. He also gave me three perfect and brilliant children. I doubt I would have discovered my unique badge of courage or my authentic self without walking across America with him.

Although Peter chose a different path than the one we started together, all human beings are flawed, and I'm chief among them. I was pathetically naive, codependent, self-righteous, and stubborn as an Ozark mule. For reasons I may never understand this side of eternity, walking across America; enduring heartache, love, and loss; and laying down my marriage was my destiny. And I wouldn't change a thing. It was tangled and messy at times, but I've learned to do two things: keep repenting and keep forgiving. God's grace will do the rest.

Now, dear reader, let not your heart be troubled. Go on your way because like me, whatever your destiny is, you are the apple of God's eye. Hear the words of my dirt-poor and sweet ole' Granny from the Ozarks: "Everything will be all right."

ACKNOWLEDGMENTS

Thank you to my immediate family and those who have lived many of the stories in this book, especially my children Rebekah, Jed, and Luke Jenkins and their families, Jonathan and Josephine Gibbs and Anna and Lyla Estelle Jenkins. And thanks to my sister, Vicky Pennell Ross, and her husband, Richard. Other Ozarks relatives who knew my parents and grandparents include Velma Crain-Crook, Cindy and Randy Heddy, Dena Matthess, Dana Miller, LeRoy and Jerry Crain, Sue Crain, Barbara Hartel, Marv and Caren Pennell, Donna and Vern Newton, Karen and John Spencer, Rebecca Farnsworth, Donna and Kenny Cox, Carolyn and Jerry Stewart, Bill Tracy, Larry and Bonnie Altenburg, and Lynne Hogfelt. Never-to-be-forgotten ex-in-laws are Winky and Randy Rice, Abigail and Jeff Boal, Fred and Colleen Jenkins, Scott and Bonny Jenkins, and Betsi Jenkins.

I have been fortunate to remain in contact with longtime friends as well as my children's friends, but I risk forgetting someone, so please forgive me in advance if, God forbid, I didn't include your name. The names are in alphabetical order: Jim and Terri Baker, Lyn and Carolyn Baker, Donald and Clara Bell, Pat Black, Connie and Toby Britton, Ann Broughton, Andy and Carolyn Burton,

ACKNOWLEDGMENTS

Sophia Bush, Stanley and Jan Carr, Pam Howison Cherry, Bridget Connelly, Glenda and Terry Copeland, Diane and David Crabtree, Phillip Crosby, Becky Daniel, Larry and Jan Davidson, Ben and the Davis Family, Margie Dillenburg, Bethel and Paul Eaker, Ashley Earnhardt, Houston and Hays Estes, Pat and Trina Flynn, Randy and Emily Fox, Elaine Ganick, Jim Ganus, Donna Gillroy, Rick and Doris Harbin, Carol Hardwick, Wally and Brenda Hebert, Kim Hickock Sky and Meaghan Hill, Bill and Laura Hendrix, Rodney and Carol Hopwood, Joan Howison, Mike and Mary Lou Koto, Deb Laffey, Ruthie Lindsey, Cynthia and Jean McClard, Viki Mammina, Renie and John McCarthy, Kathy McIver, Jim and Marcia Myatt, Jennifer Enoch O'Brien, Aaron and Lauren Paul, Rebekah and Orion Paul, Don and Erin Rahaim, Jessica Malaty Rivera, Judy and John Rodman, Paul and Beth Ruff, Ame Satterwhite, Charlotte and Terry Smith, Don and Sarah Stevens, Dr. Carol Swain, Andy and Karen Taggart, Jon and Lolita Taggart, Jimmy and Sharon Taggart, Shannon and Glenn Tomney, Betty Wayman, and Jean Wysocki.

Other Thanks

Many talented writers, agents, editors, and publishers offered comments, guidance, and constructive criticism. These include Jedidiah Jenkins, Rebekah Jenkins-Gibbs, David Knopp, Michael Palgon, Emily Barrosse, Karen Longino, Matt West, and the Boomer Girls, among whom are Emmy-nominated writers and producers. A very special thanks to Shannon Briggs for her spectacular work editing the manuscript.

284

IN MEMORIAM

Eternal thanks to my Ozarks roots and those who left solid and honorable legacies: my parents, Ernest Edward Pennell and Betty Jo Crain Pennell; grandparents, Walter Napoleon Crain and Annie Mae Watson Crain; grandparents, Forrest Truman Pennell and Viola Louise Henson Pennell. To my brother, James Edward Pennell, Uncle Victor Lee, Uncle Glen and Sue Crain, Uncle Lavell and Lillie Brown Crain, Uncle Don and Agnes Ryan Pennell, Uncle Dorice and Margaret Ryan Crain; cousins Hubert Crain, Mike Pennell, Mike Crain, Wally Crain, Dale Crain, Laveta Doherty, Jack Altenberg, and Uncle Clinton and Dee Pennell.

The list of mentors, friends, and important people who poured love and wisdom into my life include Reverend Curtis and Laverne Eaker, Jan and Bob Taggart, Perk and Emma Jean Vickers, Bill and Viola Williams, Jack and Lucy Ramsey, Tish Koto, Reverend Milo and Evelyn Franke, Homer and Ruby Martin, Preacher and Bobbie Hebert, M. C. and Margaret Jenkins, Charlotte Byrd Stack, Martha Belle Smith, Horace and Dot Murphy, Zephyr Fite, Mr. Robert George, Reverend Bruce and Lawanna (Fields) McIver, Dr. Stanley Watson, Patsy Bruce, Susan Klaus, Mickey Davis, Jim and Margie Hutton, and Reverend Charles and Barbara Green and the unforgettable Mom Beall.

ABOUT THE AUTHOR

Barbara Jo Jenkins coauthored *The Walk West* (William Morrow), which became an international bestseller and part of the permanent White House Library. A nonfiction blockbuster, it sold fifteen million copies, became a *Reader's Digest* condensed book, and was chosen as one of the most influential bestsellers related to American culture in the last 100 years. Barbara Jo Jenkins's three-year, 3,000-mile walk across America with her former husband became one of the most popular stories in *National Geographic* magazine (cover story, August 1979).

She coauthored *The Road Unseen* (Fawcett), a number-one mass paperback bestseller and winner of the Gold Medallion Book Award. Jenkins wrote *I Once Knew a Woman* (Wolgemuth and Hyatt) and *Wit and Wisdom for Women* (Thomas Nelson). She has appeared in various magazines such as *Reader's Digest*, *Today's Christian Woman*, *Guideposts*, and *Nashville Lifestyles*, on numerous national television programs such as *Good Morning America*, and on such radio programs as *Focus on the Family*.

Jenkins has been a keynote speaker at colleges, conferences, and national conventions. She has served as commissioner for two Tennessee governors, board chair for Benton Hall Academy, and president of the Tennessee Women's Forum. She is chair emeritus of the Green Electric Company and served on the board for Coaching Life Matters for people in crisis.

Ms. Jenkins lives in Tennessee and loves spending time with her family and friends. She enjoys traveling, painting, writing, speaking, cooking, floral design, creative projects, and sitting in the porch swing telling stories to her grandchildren.

Barbara Jo Jenkins can be reached at www.barbarajojenkins.com, on Instagram at @barbarajenkinswriter.

For those who wish to see original photos of the famous journey, you can see photos of scenery, people, and places on the website: barbarajojenkins.com